DWELLING

NO LONGER THE PROPERTY OF
THE ST. LOUIS COUNTY LIBRARY

POEMS

Other Books by Aliki Barnstone

POETRY

The Real Tin Flower
Windows in Providence
Madly in Love
Wild With It
Blue Earth
Dear God, Dear Dr. Heartbreak: New and Selected Poems
Bright Body
Winter, with Child

TRANSLATION

The Collected Poems of C.P. Cavafy: A New Translation

LITERARY CRITICISM

Changing Rapture: Emily Dickinson's Poetic Development

ANTHOLOGIES
A Book of Women Poets from Antiquity to Now
with Willis Barnstone

The Calvinist Roots of the Modern Era
with Michael Manson & Carol J. Singley

The Shambhala Anthology of Women's Spiritual Poetry (paperback edition of
Voices of Light: Spiritual and Visionary Poems by Women Around the World from
Ancient Sumeria to Now)

EDITION
Trilogy by H.D.
Introduction and Readers' Notes by Aliki Barnstone

DWELLING

Copyright 2016 by Aliki Barnstone

All rights reserved. No part of this publication may be reproduced or transmitted in any form or by any means, electronic or mechanical, including photocopy, recording, or any information storage and retrieval system, without permission in writing from the publisher, except in the case of brief quotations in reviews.

Designed and typeset by The Sheep Meadow Press
Distributed by The University Press of New England

Cover image: Aliki Barnstone
Author Photograph: John Farmer de la Torre

Library of Congress Cataloging-in-Publication Data

Names: Barnstone, Aliki, author.
Title: Dwelling : poems / by Aliki Barnstone.
Description: Rhinebeck, NY : Sheep Meadow Press, [2016]
Identifiers: LCCN 2016003695 | ISBN 9781937679637 (softcover : acid-free
   paper)
Classification: LCC PS3552.A72 A6 2016 | DDC 811/.54--dc23
LC record available at https://lccn.loc.gov/2016003695

All inquiries and permission requests should be addressed to the publisher:

The Sheep Meadow Press
PO Box 84
Rhinebeck, NY 12514

Acknowledgments

Grateful acknowledgement to the journals in which these poems appeared, often in different form:

Chicago Quarterly Review: "On the Occasion of Your Return," "During Drought,"
Curator Magazine: "Alas,"
Crab Orchard Review: "In the Workshop,"
Cura: "In my Closet,"
Enchanting Verses: "Winter, with Child," "Weeds,"
Great River Review: "Well," "Hummingbird Home," "Woodlands Psalm," "Holy Friday,"
Harvard Review: "Built-in," "Who Knew How Far,"
The Los Angeles Times: "Sometimes the Urge to Live,"
New Letters: "Advent," "Cats and Dogs, Whales and Frogs," "Ice Storms," "Morning Glory," "When my Greek Grandmother Came to Visit," "At the End of Your Life," "A Little More Mindful,"
Painted Bride Quarterly: "When We Were Girls in Goshen," "Elegy in the Second Person,"
Prairie Schooner: "Saunter *Sans Terre*,"
St. Katherine Review: "I Can't Remember if it Was my Dream or my Mother's," "Eat God," "Enigma Garden Café,"
Saranac Review: "Goose Rush," "Every Year the Forget-Me-Nots,"
The Southern Review: "My Greek Grandmother's Hunger."

"In the Workshop" appears in *Far Out: Poems of the 60s,* edited by Wendy Barker and Dave Parsons, Wings Press, 2015. "Alas" appears in the anthology *When Bees Are Few: A Hive of Poems about Bees,* edited by James P. Lensfesty, University of Minnesota Press, 2016. "Strange," "Meadows and Fireflies" will appear in *Thinking Continental: Writing the Planet One Place at a Time,* edited by Tom Lynch, Susan Naramore Maher, Drucilla Wall, and O. Alan Weltzien, University of Nebraska Press, 2017.

"Winter, with Child," "Alas," "Built-In," "Immigrant Hope," "I Can't Remember If It Was My Dream or My Mother's," "When We Were Girls in Goshen," "Well," "During Drought," "I Witness a Version of Salvation," "Residential Geece," "Weeds," "Hummingbird Home," and "Windows on the Past," appear in my chapbook, *Winter, with Child,* Red Dragonfly Press, 2015.

The fountain pen drawings "All Time at Once," "Bird Spiral and Prairie," "Icon," appeared in *New Letters*. Vol. 81, No. 1 / 2014-2015.

I am grateful to the University of Missouri for Research Leaves that allowed me the time to compose these poems. I am thankful beyond words for a residency at the Anderson at Tower View and for the magical synergy with my friends, director, Robert Hedin, printer, Scott King, and fellow residents Jim Heynen, Huang Zuxiang, Jessica Mongeon, and John Coy. Works in the Anderson Center Permanent Collection gave me new iconography and ideas, particularly the following:

- "Green Bird," Marc Chagall, Color Lithograph, 27" x 20", 1962;
- "Psalm I," Marc Chagall, Etching with Aquatint, 7" x 9, 1979;
- "Winter," Paul Klee, Color Lithograph, 10" x 14", 1939;
- "Taking Up Arms in the Vault," Käthe Kollwitz, Etching with Aquatint, 13" x 19", 1906,
- "Les Danseurs," Fernand Leger, Etching and Drypoint, 7 ½" x 8 ½",
- "Decoration Masques," Henri Matisse, Cut and Pasted Paper, Lithograph/Prepublication Proof, 38' x 14", 1953
- "Bacchanale," Pablo Picasso, Color Linocut, 12" x 15", 1962,
- "Chien Devant la Porte (Dog at the Threshold of the Door), Georges Roualt, Lithograph, 9" x 13", 1929.

Thank you to Ron Starbuck for help with the images. Thank you to Alex Long, Anne Barngrover, Elli Tzalopoulou Barnstone, Willis Barnstone, Beth Browne, Scott Cairns, Craig Cones, Cornelius Eady, Gabriel Fried, Monica Hand, Greg Miller, Stanley Moss, Thomas Simmons, Michael White, and Jake Young for their attentive reading and astute suggestions for revision. For playing the poetry game, which produced the majority of these poems, my joyful gratitude goes to Kathleen Crown, Ellis Froeschle, Stephanie Kartolopoulos, Lisa Rhoades, and Mimi Plevin-Foust, Rev. Cathy Rosenholtz, Barbara Rothschild, and Allison Smythe.

For my father, Willis Barnstone and my mother, Elli Tzalopoulou Barnstone,
and in memory of my ancestors from the two lineages revealed in my parents' names.

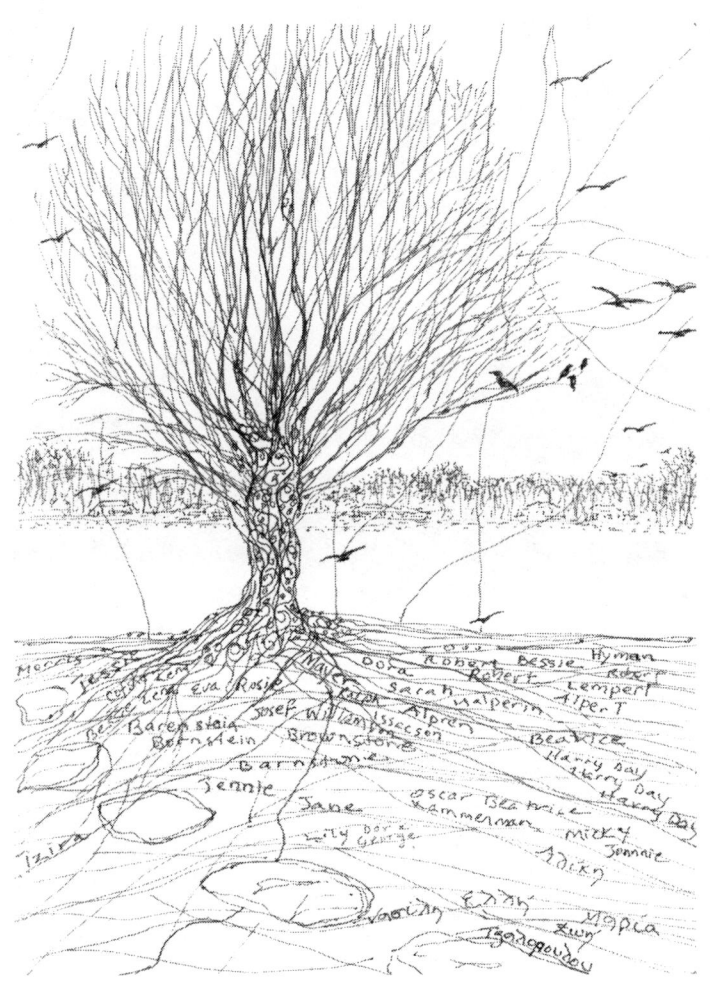

CONTENTS

SAUNTER *SANS TERRE*

HUMMINGBIRD HOME

Εκοσ Οἶκοσ

Οἶκος (*ēkos*) means house in Ancient and Modern Greek. In Ancient Greek, οἶκος has several meanings, which carry forward into the *logos* of our thought:

1. house, dwelling place of any sort (e.g. a cave)

    1. room, chamber

    2. meeting house, hall

    3. cage

    4. (*astronomy*) domicile of a planet

2. one's household goods, estate, inheritance

3. house, family, household.

In English οἶκος is the root of ecology, economy, and ecumenical.

> Ecology is formed with οἶκος "house" + λόγος *(logos)* "word," "study," "organizing principle."

> Economy is formed with οἶκος "house" + νόμος *(nomos)* "law," "custom," "principle management."

> Ecumenical comes from the Greek οικουμενικός (*oikoumenikós*), which means "concerning ἡ οἰκουμένη (*hē oikouménē*), that is, "the inhabited earth," "the whole known world," "the universe." The word ἡ οἰκουμένη (*hē oikouménē*) is from οἰκέω (*oikéō*) "I inhabit, dwell" + γῆ (gê) "earth" implied.

In Modern Greek, family, intimacy, and appropriation or ownership are formed with the root οἶκος.

> A word for family is οικογένεια, which is formed with οἶκος "house" + γενιά "generation," "ancestry," "lineage."

A word for intimacy is οικειότητα, which is formed with οἶκος "house" + τητα, the suffix for "ness" or "ity." In Greek, intimacy is "houseness" or "hominess."

A word for appropriation or ownership is οικειοποίηση, which is formed with οἶκος "house" + ποίηση "poetry," from ποιέω (*poiéō*), "I make, do, create."

BUILT-IN

WINTER, WITH CHILD
"Winter," Paul Klee, Color Lithograph, 1939

If I could have painted my soul pregnant,
we'd look like this lithograph, the weight
of my dreaming body written on stone
with fourteen lines or less. And where my hand
cradled you moving in my belly is
a bright red heart, more brightly hued than me,
the bare stick trees, the landscape, or the moon.
A ruby shape childishly drawn, a tender
symbol for you who were invisible
but felt, a part of me, apart from me,
your heart beat the iambs I could not write.
You grew in winter and the words inside
were seeds, dormant till the April you were
born, breathed, and filled your name with life, my Zoë.

BUILT-IN

I find myself in a family home, maybe in the old country somewhere,
my people gone, the rooms ordinary white—could be anywhere.

I open a small built-in cupboard, its glass covered with eyelet and lace.
It's not a shrine, though a goblet is set on iridescent silk with no tableware.

It's no holier than any other storage or hiding place, and I search for a word
same as I would a spice or a can of chick peas, though words exist nowhere.

I find no wine in the goblet, yet I drink and light shakes my upraised arm.
I'm alone, yet a crowd behind me urges, *The word, Aliki, the word is in there,*
    somewhere.

THE HOUSE MY GREAT-GRANDFATHER BUILT

He must have thought of us, the yet-to-be-born, when in 1933 he helped found the Beth Abraham Synagogue at the foot of Laurel Avenue, below the house he built, *18 Laurel Avenue,* the Victorian mansion on Auburn's highest hill, the home his children and grandchildren left for other fortunes and spoke of as Eden—their Maine R softened into an *ah* in their accents—no trace of his Yiddish tongue.

How many servants lived in the huge—at least to me—servants' quarters behind the main house? How many craftsmen's hands must have touched the abundant details? Someone—perhaps an immigrant like him—painted the cherry blossoms on the vestibule ceiling, so lovely when my great-grandfather entered, looked up through the branches, and spotted the warbler, the butterfly, and the bee lost in balms.

I wonder if he grew accustomed to luxury, though he came from Imperial Russia, a Jewish junk peddler with a funny name, Hyman Lempert. Maybe he didn't marvel each day—the carved walnut posts and barristers, the smooth banister beneath his palm when he climbed the stairs rising three high-ceilinged stories, the eighteen heavy doors that swung open on brass hinges pressed with intricate florals. When he sat in a chair upholstered with a burgundy velvet that complimented the exquisite Persian rug where gazelles danced, did he notice the parlor's beveled glass cast a rainbow on his shoe?

He was surely thinking of us and our memory of him and our people, when he gave money for the Beth Jacob Cemetery 1882, when he ordered the family stone placed prominently, the first one one sees, the largest, the polished red granite engraved with Hebrew and *Lempert* and two hands reaching from the name, holding up a crown.

Name Change

It was my grandfather's idea to change
the family name from Bornstein,
meaning *amber*

             or *burning stone* in German,
to Barnstone, also meaning *amber*.

In 1912, he, his father, step-mother,
and all his siblings stood before a judge
in Auburn, Maine,

              and Anglicized the vowels
within their name's consonants to conceal
being Jews within their souls and behind the walls
of home.

        (Shades drawn to hide Shabbat candlelight.)
The gems's classical name was *electron*,
"beaming sun," yet the Heliades grief
made them poplars and their tears golden amber.

Two centuries before, the Emperor
Joseph the Second decreed that all Jews
immediately abandon

              Hebrew names
and adopt a constant German surname.
Tax them and keep track of them like the rest
of Christendom,

           except keep the Jews humble.
No Jew may take the surname of a noble
or renowned family.

           No Jew may keep
a name if someone complains it was his.

All circumcision books and all birth books
will be in German forever and ever.

The Jews will be registered, just as Jesus
was born in Bethlehem,

           city of David,

where Joseph and Mary traveled to sign
the census decreed by Caesar Augustus.
Did the ancestors know the parallel—
register to be taxed (and rounded up later)—
when they chose lovely names: apple or pear
tree, rose, gold leaf, green field, or blooming valley?

My jeweler Zaide was a great magician
with diamonds, so I am told.
                              What if
in 1788, our ancestors
had been able to afford *Diamond*—
the hardest stone, dispersing spectral color—
would my grandfather have heard the brilliant name
as Jewish?
              and would he have chosen for us
Davies, Day, or even plain Smith instead?

Every time I look down at my left hand,
I behold
          the ring he gave my grandmother:
a platinum setting shaping a sun.
The diamond conceals
                      fire within
until, awakened by rays, it bursts
into rainbows and stars scattered on the walls
all around me:
              the covenant with Noah:
God will never annihilate us again.

Eat God

Sunday mornings
I eat God.

> The rest of the week, too,
> I eat God.

> October in the Midwest is apple season,
> and each bite announces God on the roof
> of my mouth.

> *Seraphim*
> whispers the crisp fruit
> as I chew and *chew* invites the rhyme
> and *juice* the pun.
> I like Jews, don't you?

Sunday mornings
I rise with the flock and sing hymns to a Jew
and bow to a tree
and hold out my cupped hands
for a bit of unleavened bread from heaven.

> The rest of the week I hear the Rabbi
> say the same thing he said when last we supped—

Do this for the remembrance of me.

> I take a breath and eat the whole sky
> and taste his atoms on my tongue as commanded.

Sunday mornings
the people take in God's gifts.
Oh, the body, the Body is
thin, thin as a wafer.

We get a little wine, too,
costly as blood.

The brow upon whom
God laid his oiled thumb
is the Jew's, his skin scented
with olive and balsam saved, saved,
they say, just to heal me.

The rest of the week
the Jew hangs around
reminding me,

"Eat God."

I eat an apple, which passes understanding,
and he hovers at my shoulder, out of eyeshot,
and doesn't complain about the hole in his side.

"Peace be with you," the Rabbi says.
"And also with you."

"Eat God."
"I do,
thank you."

Sunday mornings
his wine stings my throat when I speak.
An archangel's wing breaks from a cloud
and shrinks into heaven.

The rest of the week
he says, *Eat, eat, eat!*
and proves he's a Jew
(or a Greek!).

Sunday mornings
his atoms tingle my skin.

                      The rest of the week
            the gashes on his palms and feet
            don't belong to him but to me
                  and the world.
              Still they hurt him.

        That Jew dwells among us.
          Something like that.

Sunday mornings
I eat God.

                      The rest of the week
                      I dwell on God

Sunday mornings
I dwell on Earth.

                      The rest of the week
                    I wash down God
              with a little wine, spirit
       in the blood, a spill on a linen napkin.

         In an enigmatic mirror
      I see to see the Jew face-to-face.
      I can't wipe the stain from my lips.

Ancestral Home, Maine

You took the distance from me
      when you took the wheel
            and I went beyond
being the driver to being
      close to you and all I saw,
            through the windshield brightly:
my family history, the immigrant
      hope in the landscape's cells
            still indwelling,
childlike over a century later.

The sunset made the waves
      a coarse silk spread and the waters
            became a bed,
the whole indigo sky a room with ever-expanding
      walls, every stone between
            clapboard houses and boats
arranged according to the sun's eye,
      toys lost in the light.
            Evergreens and the moon
rose together from the Atlantic
      and the moon bounced
            off the trees' fingertips,
late-night volleyball, and kept rising until
      it was out of reach of
            even the highest branches.
Then we turned to each other full
      of exuberance hard-won.

COLLAGE WITH BREAD AND ROSES

James Oppenheim's poem "Bread and Roses" (1911)
was set to music by Mimi Fariña (1974).

I cannot cut and paste home, stones, the neighborhood,
      streets and stores, without a melody, without
breath rising from the pelvic floor, my humming unbidden,
      bread and roses, bread and roses.
First, the geese—and the sky the flock inscribes
      with a V on tissue-paper clouds—
and a sudden sun discloses women sometime, somewhere,
      marching, marching in the beauty of the day.

Next, gardens—a sequence of blooms glued-over, spring to summer.
      Each blossom is a fresh start, so I may forget
to eulogize the daffodils' yellow heads that withered on the lawn.
      Iris petals are torn, their inner flame cut out
separately and placed at star-angles, mimicking appliqué,
      commemorating a pretty scrap a mother stitched inside
her sick child's factory worker smock, the *"small art*
      and love and beauty their drudging spirits knew."

I save for last my attention to the needy
      roses, like us mostly non-native, flourishing
only with care, with fingers sore and skin cracked from labor.
      I cannot cut and paste my domestic scene
without the syncopation of thousands of goose honks
      and the traffic's distant groan for *"a million darkened kitchens;"*
without my hunger to eat the soup simmering on the stove
      a slice of brown bread at a table laid with roses.

I scissor and sing, *"Our lives shall not be sweated from birth until life closes,"*
      and the voices of immigrant women working the looms
in mills a century ago are transposed to today, even today—
      "ten that toil where one reposes"—the anthems and hymns

and chronicles that I snip out of newspapers (now delivered to few
        and fewer), accounts of the world, whether we're willing
to read them or not: printed on wings and bark, petals and leaves
        is the hidden work in each brick of our dwelling's façade
and in the sleeves I roll up to fit together the pieces,
        the labor of others, a history of hands.

Temperature Drop

Sub-zero cold is an ache bearable,
if only for a few bitterly walked
blue-gray moments, if you're not wearing two
worn out, soot covered coats, holes patched with duct tape,
and you don't wander with your homeless friends,
grandparents, veterans, sad love-lost teens,
hands and mouths dried by wind and lack of good
food, associated by decline, slowly
they disappear into twilight, the vacant
park where a spectral group nightly assembles.
On icy benches they layer with cardboard,
the rusted ironworks jagged beneath
their heads, feverish blood, heavy, chilled bones,
they mumble hymns into the shadows, wait
for iridescent day, hoping their tongues
taste God and bile, noses still smell stained air.

My Greek Grandmother's Hunger

When I was a child, Yiayia briskly guided
me through the streets of central Athens, grasping
my hand too tight.
          Sometimes she stopped to buy
chestnuts for me from a vendor off
Syntagma Square.
          There are churches so old
their floors are a meter below street level.

Grandfather, grandmother, and namesake aunt
were buried in the same plot in the Third
Cemetery of Athens.
          By now maybe
their dry bones are in the ossuary,
stored in dull tin boxes.
          There's an old woman
who sits on the sidewalk near the ATM,
wrapped in wool shawls and a paisley headscarf,
selling bundles of herbs.
          She blesses me
when I give her some coins and take the thyme,
mountain tea, wild sage, and oregano
and bow my head, breathing in their redolence.

"Tea, olives, and bread!" Yiayia chanted, pounding
her fist into her palm.
          "I lived on tea,
olives, and bread to get back our property
after the war." I tried to understand
but can't recall all the details.

German
officers threw olives and some crusts
from the balconies of the Grande Bretagne,
their sport to watch
                    starving Greek children fight
for crumbs or to suck flavor from a pit.

The economy collapsed and recovered.
Crises came again to the generations.

My grandmother ate when she could to stave
off famine, because to remember hunger
was to be hungry.
                    Chestnuts never tasted
so good—oh, so good—as when Yiayia fed me
toasty morsels from a waxed-paper sack.

Poetry Game
—for Dad and Blanche

I could eat the words,
      if one were "strudel."
If it were "cheese,"
      I couldn't stop myself
recalling my friends' birthday parties,
      how the farmer takes a wife,
the choosing game, and my shame
      to be the homely cheese
standing alone on a braided rug
      breathing in sour smells,

not the savory thyme and oregano,
      not the sweet
almond, filo, and honey
      of our home, my father
leaning down to read
      my page
of scrawls and doodles.
      "Bird?"
he'd ask, fountain pen poised,
      "What kind of bird?"

"Chickadee," I'd say,
      or "whippoorwill."
Their names were their songs.
      Chickadee,
his black and white head
      at home in daylight,
I could see when he sang,
      his sharpened beak writing
letters that disappeared the instant
      they were formed on air.

Whippoorwill I knew to be
      a homely bird

who sings only in the dark,
   invisibly, somewhere
in a thorny locust or fragrant pine
   so beautiful, a little
mournful. But why
   the mean picture:
whip poor Will?
   I tried to think of another pun

less punishing. If I wrote "flowers,"
   I understood to cross it out
before Dad questioned the word, unless
   it were a verb or arranged,
a bunch of flowers I'd picked
   in our field, dried up in a homely jar.
I'd say "tiger lilies," seeing
   their orange blooming
around the boulder where water pooled
   after a storm.

I'd say "hollyhocks"
   because when I crossed
our dirt road to find Blanche Bleikhart,
   I passed their sunny faces
and tall stalks propped up against
   her weathered clapboard home,
her drunk husband
   bellowing behind the walls.
I'd say "marigolds," "pansies,"
   "poppies," and "petunias,"

because she'd be kneeling in the dirt,
   humming
a hymn to the Green Mountains
   spread above her,
a velvet veil across the temple
   of sky. She looked up

and spoke with me,
        murmuring to calico
kittens winding round her ankles
        as she weeded and harvested.

I'd say "Jack-in-the-Pulpit,"
        holy and purple, appearing
in sheltered groves, because
        the bark peeled away from birches
reminded me of the lines
        of dark earth on her knuckles,
and she gently placed some seed pods
        in my young palm,
with instructions,
        a simple homily.

Because bordering the rows of homely beans,
        squash, peppers, and tomatoes,
my elderly friend raised the companion
        flowers I'd later learn
keep pests away from our food—
        and someday I'd grow
to be an old lady, gifted
        with a green thumb
and sunflowers three times as tall
        as I stand, shaded by a straw hat.

WEEDS

I like dandelions, though most say they're weeds.
In Greece they're called wild greens.
Every day the sun shines this stormy spring,

I swear I'll harvest, steam, and serve them
with extra virgin olive oil, lemon, and salt,
yet I don't make the time because I'm not

a wizard. I don't rip the minutes and hours
out of the universe by their roots
the way I used to pull up dandelions and clover.

If time were a garden and the sunset hours
the peonies and rarest fragrant roses,
the weeds, the seconds that spread

into minutes and hours, would choke the life
out of what I most cherish. Perhaps.
If I harvested the dandelions and cooked them

perfectly, I wonder if my concoction would be
eternity served on a white platter with a tall carafe
of red wine and a basket of homemade bread
to a table garlanded with all my loved ones.

MEADOWS AND FIREFLIES

Sometimes I'm an anachronism remembering the meadows
      of my childhood in the Green Mountains,
         the fireflies mirroring the Milky Way
on a moonless night, the dark almost true black,
      for miles around, the absence of light interrupted
         meekly by the two houses on our dirt road.
Acres of meadows illumined by bugs, homely things in the day
      we discovered in morning, having wandered
         with our Mason jars into unmowed grasses
and wildflowers, waist high to a child, shoulder high
      to the youngest—to emerge from the pollen-heavy
         dusky field with a lantern
of orbiting and blinking insects and to place them
      on the nightstand beside our heads, watching
         until sleep and to dreamwalk tiny,
riding the fireflies' backs, gliding beyond the glass prison
      to float beneath a cascade of golden rod,
         or alight on a downy bedspread of Queen Anne's lace.
In the tall, sheltering, necessary darkness, fireflies' bioluminescence
      attracts mates, and females lay fertilized eggs
         among the seeds on the ground's surface or just below,
and the universe in miniature sleeps in winter, to hatch and fly
      in the next year, and the next, and in all the years to come,
         could the meadows survive the future.

Not Manufactured

All the ways we play in the yard—
   a blade of grass held taut
between thumb knuckles is a searing
   whistle. We weave gold crowns

from dandelions, chanting spells
   to change our weedy selves
to monarchs. And when we crave something
   sweet, the chain-link fence is

heavy with honeysuckles. Break
   the blossom's cup and pull
the stamen out the base and taste
   a nectar droplet filled

with light rays on the tongue. The bees
   are too drunk to notice
or care we take our portion, too,
   then spin our faces toward

the sun, and stumble on the lawn,
   spreading our worthless wings
across the ground. We puzzle how
   to fly among the clouds

or perhaps the clouds themselves are puzzle
   pieces that we dovetail
or toys that cannot be made except
   with movements of our eyes.

WHEN WE WERE GIRLS IN GOSHEN
For Abigail Stone and Ruth Stone (1915-2011)

Now we're told she's buried in the orchard, though her laughter
      rises louder than the brook rushing over the rocks.
See her pointing to our lost calico cat, see her, over there,
      camouflaged by black-eyed Susans and cosmos?
She covers my left ear with her hand, saying shut out
      the voices telling you I'm gone.

She liked to sit in the peacock chair, her wicker throne. *Go play!*
      said your mother, the godmother I wished for with a dandelion puff.
When she spoke, a peacock showed off, opened the hundred eyes
      of his plumage, turning slowly all-seeing in the orchard.
Eyes of foliage domes, eyes of delphiniums and tall hollyhocks,
      we pray, guard and look over us who stitch together

with blades of grass, lilac leaf shirts and lily dresses
      arrayed for Puck's people when they come caroling
and raise up their acorn bowls,
      Heigh, ho, nobody home.
Our inside was our outside: ceiling beams, the twisted apple limbs
      slanting into wallpaper that didn't cover

only garlanded the invisible panel between this world and the next,
      the cursive tangle of raspberry branches spelling our names,
the red heart-shaped fruit dotting our *i's*,
      the wild tea roses climbing the sky,
sometimes dropping petals on the folk's tiny table—
      Meat nor drink nor money have I none—

or sometimes into their birch bark canoes
      we set afloat on the brook,

petals the color of our skin, as yet unscarred,
  petals the pages for blood sisters to write their vows upon.
Promise not to forget, we'd whisper as we swept pine needle
  brooms across the boulder, our palace floor.

We'll walk through the walls built brick by brick by the years,
  Still I will be merry, very merry.
We'll keep our dream house so clean and polish the glass so clear
  when we're crowned with feathery white hair.

HYMN FOR MY BIRD

If birds could weep, then would my tears
Let others know what are my fears.
—Anne Bradstreet

The sky is white through the old oak.
      Dark clouds glide with the wind,
whose silver glimmer rushes over
      the lake mirroring leaves.
I hope the sky doesn't turn green,
      queasy tornado sign
and say a prayer for my daughter,
      my bird, my only bird.

When she was small I kept her close
      as if nothing could befall her
shaded by my torso, my trunk,
      her pillow my arm's crook.
Now she has grown exquisite wings,
      and prefers electronics
and books over my fretting shade.
      She won't be my bird, lonely bird.

I Can't Remember If it Was my Dream or my Mother's

Once recounted, the dream runs constantly beyond
        me or her. I creep up a stone stairway, fever
pushing me higher up than I can bear to go.
        I'm afraid of heights. Far below
my cliff-walk, the lake is rimmed with mountain pines,
        and my mother stands willowy in a full skirt, calling me.
I can't catch my breath. Her voice is a breeze
        rippling the water and merging into twilight
that blurring all, exasperates me.
        I want to go to her yet keep climbing away
toward fireflies and ferns, hot and chilled—
        and still she hollers my name with the crickets,
step down, darling, step down to Mama.

        My footing's lost.
The stones are slick with moss, little waterfalls
        surround me, too beautiful, disorienting.
If only my head lolled against her shoulder or
        my cheek pressed cool against the car window,
and patches of cloud hovered over the dirt roads of Vermont,
        then slipped through the radiator grill or
beneath the carriage of our Buick Skylark,
        we'd say we're riding on clouds and hear
the tires roll onto our gravel driveway.
        The porch light would part dusky velvet curtains
and the windshield be a movie screen where maples,
        each leaf-point star-tipped, welcome us heroines home.
Then I drink the Milky Way, my mother leaning over my bed
        to shape the holy sign over me three times
and make me feel God's names hymning in my skin.

She lays a washcloth on my brow, and I breathe
her perfume, the lilies of the valley on her wrist.

My mother says fever tangled my yellow hair
and stained the dress she made me before my brother's birth.

In case she died, she said. A whirr. A seam
stitched in seconds. She works fast.

My grandmother's even hand finishes
the velvet piping around the collar, cuffs, and placket.

My buttons are askew. I can't remember
if it was my worry or my mother's, which of us acts,

sketches the scene, recalls, and calls *cross over*
from sickness to health, come back to me.

My Greek Grandmother with my Bird and at the Piano

Though she grew heavy with age, she moved
around the house in a floating waltz, singing
      Tosca's "Vissi d'arte"—"I lived for art,
I lived for love"—and pausing
to put our mess in order—she was exacting;
      she was tender—

      or to smile, bob her head,
and chirp in Greek—*poulaki mou*—
to my female canary that didn't sing
      arias like Yiayia or the sun-feathered birds
whose cages hung on whitewashed walls
on the islands and whose dreamy trilling
      filled our afternoon naps with color.

One day, talking to the bird, she whistled.
      She, who, like me, couldn't whistle.
She took my hand and we leaned our faces
toward the cage and she warbled at my bird
      that peeped and danced on its perch.

      Then we sat at the piano
and she played Chopin, her favorite, and listened
as I practiced my lesson. "Ohi," ("no") she said—
      she was exacting; she was tender—

"This is the *correct* way." I watched her hands
make music and bowed my head over the keys
      and sobbed. She stroked my head,
turned up an inquiring palm:
      "Why? Why?"
      Her beauty overcame my reply.

When my Greek Grandmother Came to Visit

When my Greek grandmother came to visit,
she got to work, painstakingly polishing
the silver candelabras she'd passed down
to us from family in Asia Minor.
She spray-starched and ironed the table linens,
pressing flat the handmade lace the wash wrinkled,
and searched through our chests of drawers and closets,
looking for clothes to mend with her skilled hands.
She hemmed my jeans, snipped off the ragged fringe
I'd unraveled myself, and was bewildered
that I wailed she'd ruined my style. I loved
my feet bare; she insisted I wear slippers.
Yet when she spoke to me, I understood
our language America made me forget.

THE SLED AND THE KITE AND THE DREAM

I dreamed I stood at the top of a steep hill,
      surveyed a valley of black trees,
          then lay on my sled, kicked
my boots back in the snow,
      and launched myself down
          the crescent run.
Wind chilled my eyes and ears.
      I plummeted
          headfirst into deep pond slush.
I feared I might freeze and drown,
      yet breast-stroking easily
          through ice floes,
found my sled floating
      next to a parchment kite,
          its tail of six ribbons—
purple, blue, green, yellow, orange, red—
      a rainbow spectrum drifting
          dark and glossy gray waters.
"My kite!" I exclaimed,
      suddenly a child again.
          No, I'd been a child all along.
I recalled I'd seen the rainbow kite
      from the hill, hovering above
          the winter trees,
and joy rose in my throat
      to hold again the ball of string
          and run barefoot
in our summer meadow,
      the calico dress my mother made me,
          flowing against my legs.
I sped downhill almost
      to my death
          to find summer in winter.

None of this makes much sense,
      the kite tugging at my hand, waving
         insistently from its realm, the sky,
except the dream turns
      the decades back, and again I am
         the girl I was, the girl I am.

Monkey Mind Goes to Fetch Something

Monkey Mind Goes to Fetch Something

I don't know if
        I'm addled or overcome
with something better
        than applesauce
or rings and a wooden comb
        lain with care
on a hammered silver tray purchased
        at an estate sale,
its metallic ripples like
        the lake on an overcast day. I forget

what I'm looking for
        because I guess things
in memory are stronger than things
        I can't keep track of. Like me, my father
loses things.
        When he gave me
the handmade wooden comb,
        he ran his fingers along the tines,
to show me
        how they're sanded smooth.

I no longer comb my hair
        except with my fingers.
My hair is short.
        Scissors never touched my dirty blond
when I was a kid bouncing
        in a tree, shaking down apples
for sauce we ate still hot
        with lots of cinnamon.
The tray's from an unknown someone's family.
        That's sad, the same way

only a few goblets
        and a tarnished cocktail shaker remain

of my grandfather's silver business
        and no one saved
the characteristically tasteful
        tableware catalogue he designed.
The diamond ring he fashioned
        for my fine-boned grandmother
is tight on my finger.
        I won't lose it as I lost

whatever it was,
        though my mind leaps, not
as my grandfather did from a roof,
        but like the monkeys in Burma who didn't
eat sweetly from my palm as I'd hoped but
        one-by-one quickly
pried open my fingers,
        bolted the peanuts
in a flash
        and swung out of sight.

My Alibi

When I forwarded my mail
    the post office misread
        my first name: *Alibi.*
I never lived in Providence
    at that address, high
        on Federal Hill. Plans
fell through. I confess to befriending
    the guys in the band who lived
        on the floor above.
        The buzzed guitarist buzzed me in—
"So you're Alibi—
    at last we meet."
And he played
    so fast
        I was altitude dizzy.

Coming Down or Rising Up

Mornings in Providence, after a weekend
of excess, my rocker boyfriend

and I walked in a lull,
having called off our terrifying *whys* for the breakfast special

and bottomless cups of coffee at the greasy spoon,
the knowing looks and almost-private joke of having communed

with a universe where even the potholes
sparkled with our illumined souls,

and we moved through a languorous Sunday dreamscape
that waking did not drape

with forgetfulness.
As yet we were blessed

with his gaze and my ease,
a momentary reprieve

from his anger and drunkenness,
my going elsewhere for sustenance.

I'd be complicit
in my own misery with every "isn't it,"

every insistent
"that wasn't what I meant."

Surrounded by others coming down
from the substance of swirling hours—

hero-weirdos, students posing as zeros in limbo—
we sat at our table by the plate glass window

where rumor might say we'd been seen or overheard.
Who cares? I willed my demeanor not to seem unnerved.

IN MY CLOSET

What a wreck of memories, aspiration, and poor
        judgment—or good if I'm fair
to myself. Any piece may be a private part
        of a dress code I assemble for public view—
just as the sacred temple undergarment is
        to the Mormon—
a tempting comparison, only I
        like black lace (or like the eyes that like
my skin beneath).

Take this designer shirt—
        cost me a song
I didn't have to sing at a Las Vegas
        boutique, a going-out-of-business sale.
The rippling gray & blue & green water motif
        is lively not flashy, the tones spot on,
enough restraint to be classy, not dull
        (oh, yes, like me—
or as I set my sights to be).

My ex touched my hip as I proudly modeled my find,
        and approved the cut
and what it hid and revealed: our taste, the shared
        proclivities we loved, then detested.
Today in my closet, unaffected, unmoved,
        I deposit the garment into the bin labeled
Upscale, a thrift shop that gifts
        vouchers to women in shelters
who need such attire for jobs and the courtroom.

Take my shirt. Let someone else make chic
        its retro-mod look, someone
who doesn't know me when she looks in the mirror,
        feeling smart.

She buttons mother-of-pearl,
        leaving the top unfastened,
a little tease, a bit of fun,
        for a weary mom toting her baby
behind the curtain of the makeshift dressing room.

Take this blazer and slacks no longer my style,
        the outfit I wore to an interview in Toronto
for a job I no longer hold.
        This sweater is prim—not me.
Stack on top every pair of toe-pinching shoes
        till my baskets are full and fill a few garbage bags, too.
Let someone else call finery and be blessed
        by my dollars misspent, my losses, and history.
I'll write it all off, come tax time.

A Rented Room In Berkeley

Five o'clock in the morning
somebody blows a trumpet,
      a few notes and he stops,
      bursts forth and stops.
And I sigh. When it's still too dark for the birds to pipe in,
why are you awake, unknown neighbor?
As for me, I worked all night, and now look out
from under blankets and ruminate
      my failures, my failures.
      Come, blow your horn
with the wind rattling the eucalyptus.
What kind of room are you in?
Will I find a house where I can stay?

Tell me, when you play the trumpet,
are you longing for home?
      Come, blow your horn.
      A door slams—oh, boy.
Soon the birds will begin to sing with you.
      A door slams again—oh, boy.
      A Cadillac shushes down
Milvia Street, a thousand streets in the name of one.
Trumpet player, your serenade has stopped.
      More doors slam.
      A car starts.
Ah, there you are, again, unknown,
playing your love to the songbirds awake now
while night sinks into the ground
and my window pales.

In the Workshop

That was the September when Berkeley was still novel
      and I took photos of my new Earth: the crowd of us
sprawled on the Plaza's brick because there on the Mario Savio Steps
      Allen Ginsberg wore a long golden tie, played his harmonium
on a plastic chair, and sang "Tyger, tyger burning bright."
      A few chosen poets stood around the sage's throne,
each taking his turn, and our friend from the workshop read
      the poem we already knew was too beautiful
and too lacerating, the tracks on their arms
      a map of shivers, the no-walls sex
they'd have anyplace, their glorious climb
      to Inspiration Point at dawn—
the sun orange enough to eat,
      uneaten oranges in their hands,
unoffered in the temple
      heroin made of their bodies.
Then their stroll downhill was more
      a free-fall or swan song over the Bay—
how mesmerizing the water's surface
      where sun-glare whirled with fathomless
blues all the way to the Golden Gate
      and anywhere they'd find
to crash—a mat of redwood
      needles, some friends' itchy mattress
in the flatlands, cardboard laid on concrete
      below an underpass near the Marina.
When he read aloud, I wanted the high
      to be metaphor: painlessness is a form
of radiance, only words, not the body
      of the poet wasting away. And if underlying
his lines we detected disease, we were helpless to address it.
      If I wanted, I'd remember what I called him as clearly
as his attentive expression and thin body leaning in close
      as I read my poem—my forgetfulness won't disturb his state—
and if he heard his name he might turn back
      to Earth from the high place where the dead go.

WHO KNEW HOW FAR

You will always arrive in this city. Don't hope for elsewhere—
—C.P. Cavafy

Who knew how far away I'd go
from my bay window in San Francisco?

I say "my" though the apartment was rented
  and I flowed from myself
   like water drunk
from cupped fingers—or perhaps
like a drunk—though alcohol's not my vice.

I sat in the window and called it home
  for a few hours, devoted
   to study, industry,
and sporadic monogamy, as if
the two words could exist on the same line.

My then-husband wandered
  room-to-room, baseball in his ear.
I absented in ink, listening
  to traffic, my soul
  roiling as my eye
followed the fog pouring over Twin Peaks
as if from the Most High's steaming tea kettle.

More than my well-chosen words,
  my lyric, he liked me,
  more than my aesthetics
eschewing narrative, he liked me
  (yes—loved me).
I liked to feel his hands on my back
  when we danced.
  He liked to feel me in silk.
Aesthetics just means feelings at its root.

Mauve was the designer color
        of the year, gracing Victorian trim:
same palette as the clouds, same palette
        as my spirit, the outer edge
        designed, maybe
with passionate hue surrounding gray area
        and my blurring, blurring the
                —unnamable I wanted numb—

and off I'd go across the bay to
another city, another conversation, another…

Forgive me. I guess
my intent was good but shadowed by hope
        for elsewhere as I was,
            who knew how far I'd go,
helpless to choose a city or a story.
His kindness was more than I could bear.

UNFINISHED LETTER FROM SERIFOS

My invitation is still open – come to the island –
        eat with me at a restaurant by the sea called Cyclops -
and share a meal, perfectly ended with sour cherries
        and yogurt and coffee to fool the dead.
In Greek, *to fool the dead* is an idiom from the Byzantines,
        and *perfect* and *end* are the same word.

And speaking of *perfect* and *the end*,
        you can't follow a commandment to forget,
though in English, we say "forget it" or "forget I asked."
        Still I give a teleological order to myself:
forget love gone bad, raise a glass to the end;
        and if you remember rapture, remember,
rapture some call the end. Don't be tempted to open
        the wrought-iron gate and hear the hinges' high drone,
a symphony (which in Greek also means agreement),
        a symphony you know by heart:
your feet touch the marble path and you find yourself
        sashaying to the cicadas' chorus,
no longer watchful, and you give in to redolence and pleasure
        and inhale the gardenia, jasmine, roses, and
memories carried in by Zephyr: the god's dare
        to lean your head on his freshly laundered shirt
and love your doom and love the risk
        you'll forget your practiced calm
because helpless kisses are a cliché made strong
        by poems whose constancy is to turn
against you, no matter the promise at the start.

...I'm sorry if I discourage your faith
        in me or my faith in me. Doubt dims
the cloudlessness that I search
        for the oversoul brooding over the bent world...

Okay, I fell again, not fell down or fell apart or behind or
        in love, except in love with the Aeolian breath.
Makes me forget I'm not young and makes sexy
        the two white sailboats crossing my window filled
with ten kinds of blue: paint and sea, sky and curtain,
        shallows in the foreground and Sifnos island
on the horizon, the horizon and my sundress,
        the deep sea and the even deeper waters
and hue—ah, you—ten kinds of beautiful blue for you.

An eleventh blue may be my memories of lovers—
        who cares that happiness was brief, like the sailboats
I wrote about that exited the bay before
        I could write down their names, gone before
I could make an illusion of the present
        present even for an instant, even to myself...

I Was Sick And You Visited Me

Once, early on, you told me in your good-
night call, you'd pray for me, a lexicon
that I withstood, unused to such ways. Rude
disease shook my cold bones between near sleep
and fever, wakening and chills. My breath
was snow on snow; my lungs sore, hollowed out
by flu. And then I felt unaccustomed
warm hands stroke my back, loosening my muscles
and mood under siege, the ache in my belly.
I felt only touch, the invisible
hands on my body healed beyond denial,
and felt it was you, you (who could not be
known), night caller I welcomed unaware.

I Witness a Version of Salvation

They very nearly succumbed to an electric smiting
      when something greater moved
the freeway traveler to see the hedge frightful
      with too much glinting and call 911.
They might have turned white hot
      and looked right in the eye of the famed ignitor,
the open-mouthed lion with inflamed tonsils,
      his mane a matted crown of burning thorns.

The angelic host sounded blasting horns and sirens
      and, ghosting across shriveled corn and soy,
woke the neighbors for miles around
      and the family inside the small farmhouse.
Firefighters hosed down drought-parched pines and grasses,
      to keep the blaze from spreading across the county,
while an almost lost circle of souls watched the flames
      die around their homestead struck by lightning.

DURING DROUGHT

Let it rain, let it rain, I chant up to clouds,
  forget a while the rest of the refrain,
    and retrace a bit of my young days

in a city famous for rain: Providence,
  a brick wall and *Eric Clapton is*
    God, the letters' slick spray-paint,

spray of rain on the bedroom window,
  desire the spring the virtuoso guitarist filled,
    notes falling on our skin.

If only love kept cycling improvisation and refrain,
  the way the musician's body keeps rounding
    to accept the guitar, and touch

deft fingers to the frets and strings, signaling
  to the nervous system *joy*
    and *endurance.* Feels good

to stay through fast numbers. Linger
  with me in shadows, murmuring
    It's the slow dance. If only

the pleasure riff kept vibrating our nerves,
  and not love's other intimate
    reprise, fight or flight,

the defenses cycling alert,
  which science says is too much
    cortisol in the blood

flooding. Let the rain be real water—
  this long drought needs a daily refrain.
    Far away the ice caps

shrink and Missouri farmers cannot
	graze their sheep, even if they are among
		the few who refuse the feedlot

and have the grace to give their lambs
	a little freedom
		though their pastures be fenced.

My garden is fenced,
	and my dogs run among sunflowers
		volunteered out of spilled bird seed.

I don't cut my grass;
	but rip it out and hope
		the wildflowers will take the lawn I hate.

Water the ones I love,
	let the others shrivel.
		Let it rain, I chant at the clouds

and forget a moment the rest of the refrain:
	let your love rain down on me.
		So sings Clapton, who moved me young.

Now the singer's older
	and wonders if his name is known in heaven,
		maybe he doesn't call out to his lover, maybe

the love who rains down on him made the mud
	and made it dry into clay cups
		so we could drink and live.

Yeah, that was then in a city famous for rain.
	Let it rain in Providence;
		let me muddle through your refrain.

SUGAR

Now I'm the kid blindfolded
      and twirled around, swinging
a bat at a piñata hung from a tree.
      No, I don't want

the candy someone else will release
      to the grass, the fruit-
flavored junk strewn with the animal's parts,
      papier-maché hooves and crepe curls of fur.

I like dark chocolate. That's it.
      The rest just rots your teeth,
makes you fat, your blood sugar shoot up
      into your mood. Sugar, your part is rage,

forgetfulness; my part, worry and dancing,
      dancing around you, or without
you, my love, though dancing with you
      is one of my favorite things

and simply remembering
      I don't feel so bad,
but worse, worst, cursed or
      that I'm wired for metaphor

and *piñata* took me to other days
      when I did not see
the blinding bleeds in your eyes,
      your highs and lows wearing me out,

killing the nerves in the hands, the feet,
      even the heart, even the brain.

Of a New Year's Eve

Maybe it's too early to think of arrival, too much
        mist across the windshield, too many opalescent plumes
                of exhaust rising from the tail pipes

of the city's revelers. We're traffic jammed, idling at red,
        waiting for ingress to a busy roundabout,
                and I have a talent for asking

the wrong questions at the wrong time, rushing clarity,
        rubbing the fog away with my palm,
                though I know my smudge will stay long after

the defroster's seared the glass mostly transparent.
        Yes, one second my mind warns it's unwise,
                the next I let escape my secret worry, ringing in

my past instead of our presence together, shivering
        on New Year's Eve. Vehicles of souls pass by,
                time flashes in our windows,

tick-tocking toward midnight: *nothing me, nothing you.*
        Nothing to do—I wonder. If I rallied
                good cheer, would you give me a smile:

"Hey, enjoy the ride!" Then maybe I'd relish the way
        you love to drive and the luxury of being
                a passenger, as sumptuous as feeling

my fingers run down cashmere sleeves,
        the warmth of my tender skin in winter, without
                even a glance or your hand briefly on my knee.

I've got no proper answer to your pronouncement, bittersweet,
        "in all your romances, the only thing that stays the same
                is *you.*" Same to you, my dear, or do I mean me?

Same ol' roundabout. You're the expert navigator
    of the ancient city's twisting streets, which are not
        a passion map: yield, one way, do not enter,

no parking, no reading mundane signs, no telling
    the scene fleeting by me. At first the cold glass
        blurs little white lights in every tree and bush

hung haphazard in a wild garden. Moments we ride along
    and then all that passes is ice sharp: bells, stars, holly, wreathes,
        and baubles. Strung in garlands of multicolored crystals

across the avenues, the wishes of the season blink
    and offer no hint the tidings the New Year will bring,
        only lit up merriment far as my eye can see.

GOOSE RUSH

The geese are gliding from the lake's center,
      lining up to hop awkwardly
onto the swath of frozen shallows near the shore
      and waddle up the hill. A few necks peek
over the crest, others peck in the grass.
      Some seem to gaze in my window
(as I gaze at them) to gauge if it's safe to cross
      into our front yard and scavenge
black sunflower seeds that winter birds
      and thieving squirrels spilled from the feeder.
I wonder if they remember the times I waited
      until a group had assembled
close by my door, languorously eating,
      and how I stepped outside with my camera,
just to capture their power in flight, and hear
      the rush of their wide wings unfurling.
If I'm an animal lover, why am I so annoying?
      I want to be in the midst of them,
the more the better, their feather-tips spread
      in silver sunlight, hundreds of wings
syncopating with their honks rising, their strangely
      sonorous chorus of warning and outrage.

ON THE OCCASION OF YOUR RETURN
—For Craig

You sit on the edge of the bed facing
        the window to our backyard and rehearse
again the old family affronts and approbation
        and I repeat the therapeutic truisms
I braced you with before your departure.

Outside the branches of the plum tree bow to the ground,
        heavy with as yet unharvested fruit,
and the dirt in the beds we enriched over years,
        turned from clay to black, is overrun
with strawberries and opportunistic weeds. I'm sorry

I unwittingly undid your work in the garden
        blind to your purposes as your family.
As the hours pass I offer you white bean and kale soup,
        chamomile tea with honey and lemon,
served with a small silver spoon, an antique,

serendipitously engraved with your initial, my kisses
        and body, a few jokes, our limbs entwined,
good sleep. Then I bring café au lait in bed
        and read you the poems I worked on
on the occasion of my solitude made all the more

delicious by your abiding love. You attend
        to my words yet observe you're left out,
and I offer that my subjects come from the daily occasions
        of our conversations, peace, and our ease—
and sometimes I listen well enough to receive a poem.

ENVELOPES

Maybe envelopes will one day
      be obsolete, maybe they already are,
yet when I was younger I delighted
      to make the vehicle
part of the letter, to make the address
      a calligraphic journey
or misspelled for meaning:
      Rose Island was once
my return, the missive's destination
      a *Blooming Town* all year round
grew from roots I drew
      from the alphabet.
And the stamps, too, I made part
      of the scene, a landscape
within a landscape or a wildflower
      among flourishing names.
Robert Indiana's *LOVE* was a billboard
      in a cityscape of block letters.
I hung portraits of my favorite
      writers, artists, and musicians
on a depot wall posted with station stops,
      and the serrated edges
were scrolled carving on a white frame.

I imagined the ones I loved
      to tell my news and thoughts
seeing my decorated envelope
      in the mailbox, not only sealed
with an ordinary kiss, but with something
      more rare that could cross over
into their care: a peony, a bluebird, a face.

In the University Library

There is no frigate like a book
To take us lands away.
—Emily Dickinson

Outside our arched window the winter sun
exits a cloud and glares downward. Inside
we practice finding a key to a door

we didn't know was somewhere in the stacks.
The floor between the shelves glimmers with decades
of wax like paths the dawn opens in woods.

Such awe. The ginkgo we read about drops
its leaves, golden fans, on our heads and feet.
The air shines with the books' orbits of dust.

We didn't know we fell asleep. We sleepwalked,
little machines in our hands, which hold
even more than our brains and even more

than the world wide web. Then to wake and open
a book (that might be so old it was typeset
by hand with real sorts) is like lifting up

honeycomb from the hive, its intricacy
revealed. Everything good that we eat begins
when the diligent bee enters the flower.

SAUNTER SANS TERRE

EVERGREENS

Evergreens. The name's abstract and deep colors
recollect meandering paths somewhere
in childhood, my parents close by.

The name abstracts my family—all of us are agéd now.
The winter daylight polishes pewter ground,
snow and trees, or else nothing gleams at all.

Those evergreens along a path are somewhere
in childhood, my parents close by, my brothers
leading with sticks upraised as if they held
the power to show the way.

I'm agéd now and meander on my path,
so many things left undone:
the evergreens I did not plant along
our dreary chain-link fence.

Winter daylight polishes pewter ground
and recollects our meandering on paths where thorns
of blackberries caught our clothes and bare shins.

Some days nothing gleams at all.
Some days recall the evergreens' blue shadows
shading us in feathered sun, wild blueberries
growing in acidic soil between the cracks
of lichen-covered boulders.

I'm agéd and lament things left undone.
Evergreens. Their cool shadows feathered the sun
and we ate fruit as we walked, staining our lips.
A mammoth sunflower hangs its shriveled head.
I should have planted a wall of blue spruce.

ELEGY IN THE SECOND PERSON
—*for Cliff Becker (1964-2005)*

Some say the pronoun is abused above all in addresses to the dead.
That would be you, dear friend. But if I don't talk to you, I pretend

some golden bangles aslant on a stranger's wrist don't have me
admiring your daughter's drawing, pulled from your breast pocket,

a pencil sketch of a dinosaur, a tractate in French carefully printed below,
her young hand still unused to writing, though too soon she'd be reciting

"Nothing Gold Can Stay" at your memorial. She loves gold—you doted on her so.
Some say too much. Too much, too soon your heart let you down, down

to the floor, mid-sentence as you spoke with your girl. I wonder what you said.
I don't expect your answer. On second thought she recited "Reasons for Moving"

in your memory. The gold poem fit the jewelry you delighted to give her.
You see why I need to keep talking to you? If I keep your name lodged

always in my throat, ready for you to hear, you'll be bold and tell me
a raunchy joke and laugh at your badness. If I've forgotten the punch line,

it doesn't matter. I'm doubled over—*oh, Cliff, oh, you, oh, Cliff.*

WELL
—for Cliff Becker (1964-2005)

Well, no precipitation today.
        Where I wonder
                does the interjection *well* come from?
Perhaps well-wishing and blessing?
        A pause, throat-clearing,
                or a dismissal?
Some wells plumb the earth, some well up in the soul.
        When I was a kid, a well
                near the lilac hedge was our source.
When the pump went, no water.
        When the sump-pump went, a flood
                in the basement.

And what about well-and-good—
        is that overkill?
                Or oversoul? A little love ditty
to catechize kids with the all-wellness and all-goodness,
        of God above,
                whose name that is not a name
suggests itself whenever I talk to you
        as I am now,
                downcast and angry
that you aren't answering,
        and those who love you can't agree
                what you want from us.
Or am I overcast unlike the autumn sky today
        when the prediction is zero chance
                of precipitation.

Acorns and leaves—
        are they precipitation, too, in fall
                when chrysanthemums give
color to yards? The unusual snowy mums brighten
        the bordering rust and bronze. I think
                the white is absence

63

intensifying presence, but white is all color,
        so my correspondence fails,
                and the flowers aren't untainted:
some petal-tips are tinted lavender,
        the hue of another perennial,
                sweeter smelling. Too bad it didn't rain,
and the rain didn't scent the atmosphere
        with winter coming on.
                My garden needed water.
Too bad
        precipitation didn't match my sadness.
                I cried only when I cut
onions, and those tears hardly count
        when counting sorrows. Why in hell
                count sorrows? Just to feel sadder?

Well, all day I've missed you and wished
        for rain to absolve me of neglect
                that precipitates plant death and self-
annoyance, if such a thing exists, because
        after so many years, rage against
                death is too strong or at least a cliché.
Why did you die young? Did your self-neglect
        precipitate your demise, as exemplified
                in the dictionary definition? Or was heart attack
double-helix scripted in your genome?
        Who knew you weren't well
                when last we spoke, tracing a dream
itinerary to Athens and Alexandria,
        never dreaming our families would eat together
                as we'd planned, on the Mediterranean sea,
only without you, except as ash held
        in your wife's and daughter's
                gold lockets.

ICE STORMS

The ice storms stop us, keep us
    home, if we're lucky, looking out
        windows, still surprised
by our helplessness when we listen
    to routine reports:
        planes grounded,
schools closed, brutal, spinning
    accidents; and the shame:
        a few homeless buried in snow
until the thaw; dogs left outside
    bark for love and shudder
        until their breath freezes.

Outside my window the snow
    glows with the purity
        of zero-belows,
one ice storm following another.
    Yesterday's gray afternoon
        added a new, untouched inch.
The lake is completely iced-over
    and snow-covered, almost without
        shadow. I can't look at such white—
dazzling and flashing—without
    squinting, as if the frozen lake stole
        fire from the sun and made itself
a small cold star on the ground,
    a gleaming up to heaven
        or amassed flames from the center
of the Earth and froze heat
    into iridescence, a huge fire-opal
        surrounded by violet shadows
of human enterprise: homes
    and sleds, streetlights and roads,
        shade trees planted long ago

whose thick branches snap
        with the weight of long icicles
                formed by a water-main break,
shooting and spraying for hours,
        soaking workers bending in mud,
                freezing their clothes almost
to stone. On their exposed skin
        a red sheen spreads feverish
                translucence, burns their hands.

AT THE END OF YOUR LIFE
—for Bill Russell (1929-2010)

I wanted to write down some moments,
      sitting in our friend's yard,
          but now they're gone.
The minute-hand on my watch spun them away,
      the diamond chips that mark the hour's intervals
          glimmering on a crow's wings
and on the ash tree already in winter
      when he lands. Perhaps I should have written
          where instead of *when he lands,*
but these days you confound space and time. Like love.
      As love does. As in *Love is strong as*
          death, the word I don't wish to say.
And saying it, I note now
      I shift to the present tense. We're waiting
          for our mutual friend to come home.

"Ah," I can hear your fond cadence, "mother and daughter."
      Zoe and I, side-by-side on a wrought-iron bench,
          are waiting to sing.
I want to write you a sanctuary,
      a circle within circles.
          My arms encircle my child
and she leans her head against my shoulder
      and the scents from Mary J's herb pots enfold us
          and the leaf-strewn grass rings the concrete patio
and the uppermost branches surround the crow perched
      in the ash tree already in winter enclosed by a wall
          of trees back-lit with slanting afternoon sun,
the leaves vivid with autumn, autumn that speeds up time
      with daily changing beauty: "Heavenly hurt it gives us,"
          our favorite poet observes from her room
during the Civil War. "Are you in danger?"
      Emily secretly writes in pencil to her abolitionist friend.
          Her eyes are failing; the physician took her pen:

"The only news I know
        Is bulletins all day
                From immortality,"
the "Flood Subject." "No one could evade
        the war's spreading stain," its Circumference
                widening in Consciousness
as she composed
        at her surprisingly
                small table.

I'm starting a new stanza because we need a break
        from earthly hurt: we descend to dirt
                and become heavenly dust;
because *stanza* comes from *room*
        or *abode* in the Italian, and I know you delight
                in etymology. Maybe a sanctuary
is where fugitive spirits withdraw to be kin
        with small creatures scanning the circumference
                for danger: here where I sit with Zoe whispering,
'See, the squirrel looks like a fox, with its big, rust-colored tail."
        "It's fat," I say, "fat from acorns."
                "No, its tail is really fluffy and healthy."
Beyond our quiet conversation,
        the squirrel, and the crow,
                beyond the tree wall turning
gray-green as sun sets,
        a siren sings a solo
                backed up by traffic's high-hat hiss.

Mary J arrives in this stanza to give us voice lessons,
        and while Zoe sings I wait in her study,
                addressing you with the rainbow array
of markers she uses to write
        devotions at the crack of dawn.
                Crack of dawn, odd phrase,

as if the sky were indigo glazed ceramic
       that the morning hour drops
            and shatters with wings aflame,
as if each new day enacted the vision of Rabbi Isaac Luria,
       the Kabbalist who discerned the twenty-two holy letters
            that built the world,
the twenty-two vessels that could not hold the Light
       at the beginning of time, and fell to Earth
           and left our being nonsense and shattered,
our light in the splinters, left us
       to invent glue with love,
           or whisper connective tissue to life
or raise up the sparks that remain with each encounter.
       Tikkun Olam. To heal the world. I'm trying to
           write you (write
to you,
     for you,
        of you).
I can't find
       the preposition to hold you here,
           elusive part of grammar,
word showing the relation of a noun to another word,
       word that might attach the twenty-two holy letters to sense,
           that might bond the shards we are to God.
I write to bind you to our moments darkening into shadows, sustained
       whole notes lengthening into evening, as if time swelled
           its lungs with night air in concert with Zoe singing
in the next room. I want you to hear her with me
       as the call comes through the door,
           along with the past I recall now.

I put my notebook down for my turn to lie on the floor,
       make my voice into a siren.
           "Why - do they shut me out of heaven?"
Emily asked, "Did I sing – too loud?"
       Still I ascend higher,
           higher than I know,

where I fear to go—
        I mean, feared to go until she taught,
            "Become a child again."
You would've laughed
        and quoted the scripture almost as a joke,
            to enter the kingdom of heaven,
if only you'd witnessed me be a girl again, silly,
        my breath rising free,
            and my throat forgetting to catch the air
going to my head, vibrating in my temples,
        you'd hear me hit the high notes,
            the sirens' yowl. I say the sirens
not to be poetic or evoke Odysseus' adventures
        but because their alarm jolts us out
            of calm rooms.

Beyond the wall of trees
        down Broadway, ambulances race death
            to the hospital, where for a few days
you and your wife, Mary Faith, lay in separate rooms,
        in your "life-threatening conditions," as they say.
            (I've lapsed into the past again, I'm afraid.)
Remember, you said, "I expect to be lucid a few more weeks,
        a little loopy from the morphine but lucid.
            I hear the stones cry out, so I must be loopy.
But I always heard them cry, just as our Lord said,
        for lack of the world's praise."
            "Loopy and lucid is good," I said,
standing up so we were face-to-face
        (you're tall even sitting on the edge of a hospital bed)
            and looked in your eyes, "Still a lot of light in there."
Still a lot of light in there
        might be a good last line for a poem
            but like Walt, I'm not ready to stop,
now that the stop in my throat has been loosened.

I want another stanza,
              not a hospital room,

a living room, yours and Mary Faith's, opening to your balcony
              and garden in pots, petunias spilling onto tiled floor,
                            zinnias and morning glories rising through the balustrade
overlooking the Uprise Bakery and the Ragtag Cinema,
              good names, good signs
                            of our town, which at this moment appears to me
a play town, a little mystery play, even given
              the hungry and homeless
                            who sleep on church floors on sub-zero nights
and the plaque on the Missouri Theater declaring
              Lest we forget / Never again!
                            the WHITES ONLY front door,
a play town, a little mystery play, even given
              the *Missourah* inherited from the Confederacy.
                            You shook your head and cried with shame
when you told me you were a little farm boy
              raised with a black dog named Nigger.
                            You told me about a slave named Sarah
—or was it Sallie—on the wagon train from the East.
              Without her your ancestors could not have survived
                            the journey from Virginia, half-way across the continent
and she made a *way in the wilderness* for the generations
              and for you to be born. She might have been
                            your great-aunt or great-great-aunt—
I don't remember. Forgetting is the shame
              of mourning, the *mortification* of the living,
                            and I don't know if you recounted history
to unburden your wings, "off Banks of Noon"
              and "leap, plashless" in Emily's stanza,
                            whose root is the Latin, *stay* (where the sun is
at its apex and there is no time). Or did you tell me, hoping

I'd remember, believing I'll be living for a while
        off the Banks of the Missouri River

or near the place where you and Mary Faith
     consider the lilies of the field
         and give up cars to live
on the second story of the old Central Dairy Building,
       downtown where you can see students at the Uprise,
         hunched over their laptops, maybe a mug
warming their hands, and wafting up to you, murmuring
       conversation about a film at the Ragtag,
         the cash register ping, fragments of music,
clink of tableware and wine glasses, the smell of bread,
       a little communion in the air,
         along with commerce and goings-on,
and the comings and goings of your friends,
       who climb the stairs to your apartment.
         You open the door
to your own *stanza,* your own *abode,* which in Old English
       was the past tense of *abide,*
         abide in me as I abide in you,
and I pray, "Stay, stay, stay."
       You tell me some old friends came to visit.
         "I was sick and you visited me,
since you know I'm dying."
       You wink.
         Be of good cheer.
And as they left, they told a joke you'd love to repeat:
       "Let's hope this is the first
         of many last goodbyes."

MORNING GLORY
—*for Bill Russell (1929-2010)*

The morning after you died, we considered
the lilies, as you did, faithful for us, though frost
would have withered the lilies' silky petals.

When your breathing stopped, frost crystalized our town,

as if another breath took over where you left
off. Frost on the windshields and on the died-back grass
of our backyard knoll, frost a filigree silver

halo around the burning bushes whose globes contained
a few red leaves still flaming in mid-November:

my window framed an icon of the Pentecost
in Ordinary Time. Here chickadees hovered
at the feeder, caps brilliant black and white, their song's

insistent humor—*dee-dee-dee*—recalled you,
and your eminence was in the cardinal's searing

whistle. I heard your play: his crimson mitred head
could as easily have made him Episcopal.
An athletic squirrel dug fast and filled his jowls.

When you were sick and we visited you, you rose
to greet us and held each of us and let us go.

"Even though I'm ready to go home to the Lord,"
you said, "some nights I hear the stones' cries and wake."

Here's the picture I snapped of our stepping stone path—

morning glory blue in the sky, morning glory
on the lake, blooming everywhere now that you are
out of season, past seasons. Is that where you are?

Did I take a picture of you on the morning
of your glory, on the morning after you died?

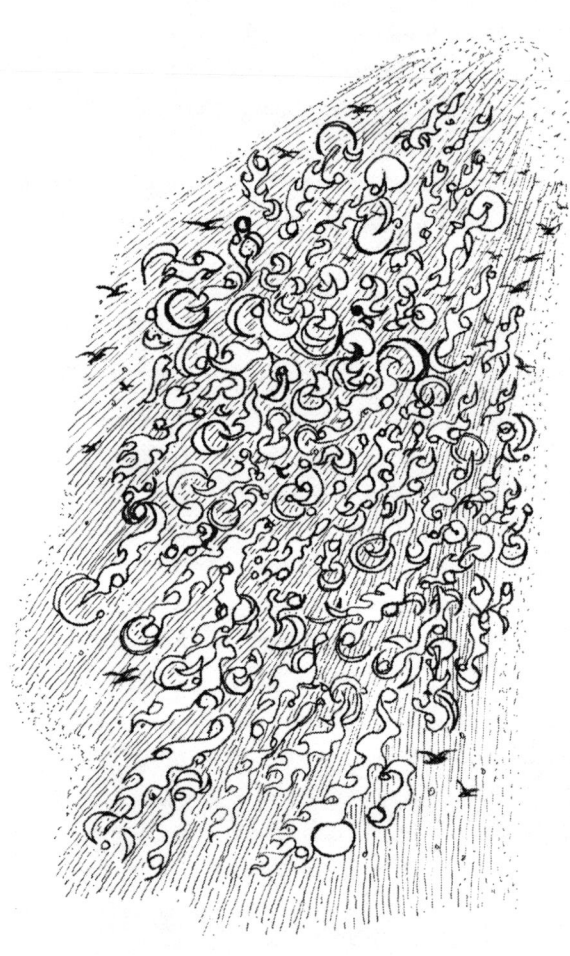

Residential Geese

Maybe morning's a happy deception.
The frost vanishes when it glistens brightest
and wakes the windows from their despondency,
the winter narrative. Through the cleared glass
a dream is building on the silver waters
a mansion made of leafless trees and fog,
turrets of evergreens, the residence
of Canada geese that were never taught
to migrate, descendants of the endangered
who were raised captive then released
into a warmer world of man-made ponds
and lawns, suburbs laid out for a goose banquet,
with lots of grass to eat. No room for wild
red foxes, wolves, bears, snowy owls, bald eagles—
so, safe and peaceable with deer, the geese
couple for life and multiply. As ever
in V-shaped formation, by instinct ordered,
they fly in symmetry across the water
that's unfrozen mostly, and is unlike
winters before. They poop on docks and rafts
and on the beach's trucked-in sand (refreshed
each spring), annoying human residents,
who search the shore for nests made of dry grasses,
lichens, mosses, and lined with down and feathers.
Warding off watchful birds with canoe paddles
or sticks, they paint the eggs so they can't hatch.
This morning geese waddle in procession,
a loopy dance, punctuated with honks
and wings up-raised, half-spread. They mount the hill
and stepping stones leading up to our door.
Assembling like portly persons in suits
the geese seem to be peering in the windows—
until I'm seen. Their wings' power unfurls
and lifts their awkward bodies up to be
the V writing their beauty visible,
the whole sky taken with its formation.

Enigma Garden Café

That was the parade of the desert, the way
        an acrobat was a small cloud,
                wings loosing sequins to heaven,
as it leaped to a trapeze
        that was on second glance
                in the rearview, a bar
across the freeway, holding signs
        that should have told me
                my direction—
even a skeptic like me,
        slyly pressing color
                to my lips
at the traffic lights—
        & then a thin line
                on my eyelids—
that was a form
        of preparing my heart
                for the crowd or a single person
standing in the doorway
        to the Enigma—
                now closed—
where Christmas lights spiraled
        round the Joshua trees & palms
                all year—
& a surprisingly large circle
        of the faithful gathered weekly
                to hear word-art—
interrupted
        by the newborn's coo,
                babble, what-not
sounding out—forget silence,
        forget everything.
                Listen: abundance.

ADVENT

Some nights sleep walks across the lake and
lays its peaceful palms on the eyes of others:
       Rest, rest.

I'm left like Eve after she ate seedless fruit, knowing
what she should not know, hearing God walking
       with wind in the first garden.

Here the winter wind carries the voices
of my beloved dead from the other shore,
       murmuring among themselves—

and sometimes even humming and caroling grow nearer
and I turn on all the lights so I won't see
       their faces gathering hope at the windows.

Rocking Chair and Moon and Saint

Sometimes I sit in the rocking chair too large for my feet to touch the floor, and I look up at the face of the man in moon, whose mouth is always open.

Sometimes he opens his mouth, joyous and surprised, and sometimes he grieves. Sometimes he lectures and other times he laughs at riddles whose words I can almost hear.

Sometimes he is a she and is me, my face in the mirror.

On the moon's way up the summit of sky, the sycamore catches its face in its arms, its eyes searching for heaven, like the statue of the saint in our living room, Saint I-Don't-Know-Who my parents found in an antique store in Spain long ago.

We used to be compatriots and I let him hold my doll in his outstretched arms until I grew taller and no longer stood with him face-to-face, no longer came close to look in his amber eyes. The saint whose name I forget stares at my bare feet, then at my hands on the armrests, as I rock back and forth, back and forth in the huge rocking chair.

Sometimes the moon chatters about the stars I can't see (blanked out by house-light). Sometimes the moon sings me a lullaby in Spanish (and I hum along, trying to recall the words someone sang to me, before the saint shrank away and became stiff painted wood with colored glass eyes.)

Sometimes the shining face looks down on me without a word, though I hear a chant in a minor key:

> I'm alone and not alone,
> lonely and not lonely.
> Someone is close by, close by.

I'm awash in moonlight, rocking, rocking in the enormous chair.

DRAWING THOUGHT

I listen to what I see—

my lines rise steeply,
　　　　as I climb above whitewashed walls,
　　　　　　　　sailboats in the bay, salt on my lips

and in my throat,
　　　　one stroke rhyming
　　　　　　　　with the stroke I draw beside it.

Here's a marble fountain, water
　　　　spouting from a lion's mouth,
　　　　　　　　eloquent, quenches my thirst.

In the chair beside me my beloved looks on:
　　　　"Right there—I see a face
　　　　　　　　you haven't drawn."

Her jawline, nose, and dangling filigree earring
　　　　I clarify in ink. Her hair is a mountain
　　　　　　　　or a waterfall flowing

from a light-blanched source, as if
　　　　from nothing, wild and elegant
　　　　　　　　coils, curls, and beads,

her peaceful eyes and half-smile ready to speak
　　　　a lexicon I call
　　　　　　　　"Big Dreams."

THE GREAT ALONG
—*for Michael S. Harper (1938-2016)*

Ah, Michael, I follow "the great along,"
      recall climbing the steps
           of Horace Mann Hall (not slipping
on ice made rough by salt),
      the heavy door's weary yowl,
          smell of old wood,
smell of old books,
      balsam
          to stave off forgetting
the seminar room.
      You entertain questions
         yet demur
answering directly, multiply questions,
      improvise, correct
         "miseducation."
We listen to your mystery
      and the imperative to read history,
         as poets, artists, and musicians
transmit it. The way,
      dear Michael, is 40 years past.
         I tried to follow along.
Was I headstrong? Or did I rush
      head long into your dream,
         a love supreme,
those nights (drawing close
      to the heater's blue flame)
         I painted music?

Winter days
      (and *those winter Sundays*)
         revolve into spring:
slush warms into mud at the roots.
      I hear you say,
         photosynthesis,

the sun powering buds and shoots
          to become magnolia and rhododendron
                    blooms overcoming
wrought-iron and chain-link fences
          alike, all over Providence.
                    Provide, provide
  the path "where we don't want to go,
          we're not prepared to go.
                    The musicians take us instantly there."
Ah, Michael, you die May seventh.
          Am I to follow the sound
                    Coltrane plays you into heaven?
Poplar leaves in the wind,
          birds crossing my window:
                    notes from the other side:
your chanting voice,
          your slant rhymes.
                    Hydrangeas
sigh

     strange

          jazz:

Four Women Talking and Writing

There's a view of a field and a stand of poplars
lovely in their bearing nothing
but winter sun.

The trees' ink scrawls on far blank sky,
as translucent as the thin blue aerograms
we filled with autobiographies of our foreignness.

That correspondence is somewhere…perhaps
in a box deep in a closet that stretches under the eaves
of a childhood home, left and forgotten

by a younger self, also mostly left and forgotten,
whose hands were deft not stiff, who tried
too hard to be loved, and did not talk to the dead.

Keenly that young woman is recalled, yet quickly
given up—a pair of cardinals flash across the glass,
pause at the feeder, and we murmur

in our easy chairs. The branches split into smaller
and smaller characters, phonemes I can't hear,
letters I can't read except

as likenesses of the losses of my friends
who sit with me, quietly confess stories, give balms—
Oh and *Ah* and *yes*—ask questions. We list some words

for play and bow over notebooks. (Later we read, if we like.)
One of us shifts in her chair to ease pain,
gazes out the picture window—and again, she writes.

SAUNTER SANS TERRE

How womankind, who are confined to the house still more than men,
stand it I do not know; but I have ground to suspect that most of them
do not stand it at all.
—Henry David Thoreau, from "Walking"

Henry David Thoreau, whose birth name
      was transposed, David Henry, wrote "Walking,"
            how to get lost and find yourself awake

on the Earth without borders, for to saunter
      was to be "*sans terre*," an itinerant
            "without a land or a home, but equally

at home everywhere," a Holy-Lander
      emerging from the mist without a map,
            having forgotten everything learned by rote.

Henry David Thoreau (David Henry) was a narcoleptic
      and opened readers' eyes yet couldn't help
            closing his, and stepping through the mirror

into the reverse forest of dream:
      a pair of indigo buntings land
            iridescent on a deer path unmarked

even by gravel—flashes of indigo, spectral color,
      appear in the air before a wanderer's eyes—
            and their tiny shining

casts a spell upon attention. Then they land
      and peck between pebbles
            and leaves for some seeds to eat.

Henry David wanted men to wake up
      in "absolute Freedom and Wildness,"
            "part and parcel of Nature,"

in a landscape not partitioned or owned
        by gentlemen multiplying fences,
                keeping their "pleasure-grounds" private.

Thoreau, who might doze off into his soup,
        berated the State: "half-witted...timid
                as a lone woman with her silver spoons."

Yet lone women read his essay about a night in jail,
        "the only house in a slave State
                in which a free man can abide with honor."

Thoreau fell asleep for good before his "Walking" made it
        into print, before he could see the counterpart
                in his dream—"some part of us

awakes which slumbers all the rest of the day
        and night"—who, *sans terre*, by law
                owned by father and husband, became

a Holy-lander of the soul:
        "out of such wildness comes
                the reformer, eating locusts and honey,"

uncivil, disobedient, strong-boned—
        a woman sauntering far,
                far from the confines of the home.

HUMMINGBIRD HOME

MOTHER-DAUGHTER TIME

I adore my daughter,
      so similar we cross borders
of time and trade places. I'm old enough
      to have crossed the ocean
in a ship, when I looked like her,
      and she's old enough to vacillate
between accepting my tender offerings
      and turning her face from my kiss.

She might be making our movie
      on the screen in her hand:
she stands on the dock,
      waving a red cloth,
a silk headscarf, perhaps, or
      a plain cotton napkin.
I see her urgent banner above the crowd,
      her face bright in the wind.

All the others surrounding her—
      who are they? Are they
the friends with whom she shares
      her portion, willfully
blind to me? The crowd moves, by turns,
      as one blur, a cloud or a stormy sea,
impersonal, and by turns, focused
      souls who also adore their kin, émigrés,
parents and grandparents who sail
      to and from the other shore.

I lean over the ship's rail,
      having been lifted
from chronology, not knowing
      if her upraised arm greets

my arrival or waves goodbye,
     just as these days every hello
echoes the goodbye soon to come
     when she leaves home.

Windows on the Past

I must have written these lines on a gray autumn day,
       knowing the way darkness falls, as the expression goes,
like a shade drawn across the window too early
       one day, and earlier the next, steadily dimming
the illumined clouds that released angels in summer,
       whose wingspans grew too wide and whose spirits
became the fog gathering in the churchyard I saw
       through the window. I'd stand against the wall
just to keep standing, feeling worse than melancholy.
       I wrote, "a sugar maple is inflamed with its own color,
with expansive yellow passion" —the desire
       of a younger woman in a sad marriage
I'd rather not remember. When music on the radio
       was beautiful, I thought, "none of this is new,"
not even a flute painting in my mind's eye:
       Chagall's swooping brushstroke encircling the lovers
in a protected, unbroken globe, a huge green bird
       perched above, or Matisse's dancers, hands clasped,
circling fast, each one reaching for the other, leaning
       into the momentum of their shared joy,
or the tender hands of mother and child portrayed
       so often. "None of this new," nor is the prayer,
"let none of these be harmed." If only such human-
       made marvels could save us, be our mirrors,
the promise of the saints, as the holy icons are
       our windows opening to heaven and a new earth.

I count the years to recall—that was which war
       or which eve of war? "If the air is still and a leaf drops
through an unmoving tree, it's because it's tired and it's time."
       What a bleak parable, I must have penned numb, too weary
to "lay aside every weight," as St. Paul tells his fellow Jews,
       and "run with patience the race that is set before us."
Why is the question, "when will I find peace?"
       fixed on the self, not on beyond? I hold my head,

heavy as the world in my hands, and mutter words, futile,
      I suppose, against the murderous judgments of leaders
who have their own words based on scripture,
      and who swear—so help me, God—just as I do,
and hope to join our voices with "so great
      a cloud of witnesses" as encompasses us all.

A Little More Mindful

Busy yourself with your daily duties, your loom, your distaff…
for war is man's matter…
—*Iliad, Book VI*

If I could be a little more mindful,
      groom my dogs' fur, remember
            to shelve my books, shut the closet
and cabinet doors, hide away
      my mess of clothes and dishes,
            and graciously address every annoyance
(or worse than annoyance), perhaps
      my sandals would glide up marble steps
            and I'd find myself idle,
holding my peace, my desperate
      thoughts left to themselves
            at the bottom of the hill, while I turnover
in my palm some stones that hold
      the spirits of those who do not cry out
            praise for a king riding a donkey,
clothed in garments his mother wove,
      her design covering his flesh from birth
            until he hugged his shroud
on a road strewn with rags and palms
      and wept over the city:
            "If only you knew
on this day those things creating peace."

Centuries before his word, their spirits dwell
      in rubble, for countless wars
            knock stone from stone.
They perished so long ago, their wanderings
      and homes are the work
            of archeology. Their pots are dust
the Athenian shopkeepers sweep away
      each morning, along with the art
            of their looms: the saffron

and hyacinth yarns spun for the owl,
      chariot and wingéd horses
            on Athena's raiment, the story-cloths
on which the Fates dance and lament,
      and teach child-bearers
            to weave defiance in a double purple web,
their textile and text incomprehensible to men.
      Soldiers cannot divide the seamless robe
            passed from mother to daughter,
mystery in a single thread.

GETHSEMANE PSALM

After they ate the Seder meal, whose order is very long,
        they sang the closing psalm, and walked together
        until they came to the grove.
Jesus prayed for them and still wanted to talk
        to his students, his friends.
The rhododendrons closed their petals;
        the blood red poppies in the fields beyond
        had faded at twilight.
Jasmine, thyme, cedar, and chamomile scented
        the dark air of Gethsemane.
The adolescent boys and girls, who'd eaten and drunk a lot,
        were exhausted with the hours, bearing
        the history of the Jewish people,
        and they slept beneath the canopy of olives.
The cyclamen stood sentry beside their black curls,
        like birds bowing their heads, balancing
        on one leg. "Stay awake with me
        and pray," their Rabbi said.
Even loyal Peter, who blurted out his every thought,
        was drooling on his pine needle pillow.
In sorrow until death, Jesus was human and afraid,
        wanted comfort and company to endure
        the torture Pilate ordered for the tens of thousands
        who dared rebel and love the poor.
"I am the way and the truth and the life," he said,
        yet he anguished: *no praise for my deeds.*
        I'll go to the trash heap of skulls,
        like the other insurgents and thieves.
"Stay awake," he whispered to their slumbering forms
        sleeping off their feast of flesh and blood,
        though he knew—as He knows all—that to wake
        and see him fully human and fully God was more
        than could be borne by these beloved children.

Sometimes the Urge to Live

Sometimes the urge to live
      seems like a crime, as if
      my absence would save
a family from a bomb or keep
      their tiled roof intact
      or the stucco from cracking
and the cinder block walls
      from smashing
      into ash and dust.

Under their vulnerable roof,
      a mother holds a spoon
      at her toddler's lip,
and a lithe teenage boy sways
      in the corner of the room
      to music only he can hear.
He's a nimble dancer, spinning
      a loose-limbed dream partner,
      his muscles too sinuous,
his dark hairline too even,
      his curls too tight
      for blood to mat and tangle.

The grandmother finishes mending,
      sticks her needle
      in a red pin cushion.
"Aren't you hungry?
      It's time to eat."
      We all want to feed our kids,

sit across the table, watching
        their gestures as they talk
        and handle silverware,
holding an instant safe in memory,
        something private and unspoken
        that won't be etched
on a plaque in a future decade,
        with words like "martyrs"
        and dates and numbers dead.

HOLY FRIDAY

After he gave up his spirit, the dogwood grieved
    that it was strong and straight and heavy,
    chopped down and crudely made to be
    the tall cross he dragged up Golgotha Hill.
He blessed the tree that was only fulfilling the scriptures,
    that had no will and yet could feel,
    and shriveled and shrank crookedly in shame.
He blessed the tree and suddenly
    the dogwoods all over the Earth
    bloomed white or pink, luminous
in twilight, a little thornless crown at the center
    and four fleshy petals for the points of the cross.

And a robin landed on one branch
    to announce the spring,
and a mockingbird landed on another
    to repeat the good news,
and an owl landed on another to wisely chant
    a lament for the dead.

Then the ground trembled and opened,
    the archangels flew out of the immense
    waning red Passover moon,
    and flanked him as he descended into the underworld.
And the sage and thyme and rosemary
    growing close to the ground
    released their fragrance as they were trampled
    by him who would trample death,
who pushed aside the granite stone covering the tombs
    and took Eve and Adam by the hand
    and pulled them bodily from their graves.
The first mother and father shouted out to be risen,
    on their feet, held in each other's arms,
    touching heart to heart, and testing
    the muscles in their fingers.

The owl was heard solemnly chanting praise;
the mockingbird repeating the good news;
the robin announcing the spring.

Yet he would not be interrupted, the cattle and sheep,
winemakers and bakers, farmers and shepherds,
and the loyal dogs leaning against them,
the weavers and the barefoot children died too soon,
and women exhausted with birth
found themselves upright, standing witness
as all the souls were good
after their original nature.
Even the warrior kings and even the rich,
killers whose gold starved the rest,
these, too, he allowed into the cloud.
He let them be poor and naked and sick,
let them hold a dogwood branch as a scepter.

ALAS

All the days since the spring equinox
        I've been unable
                to get the word
alas
        out of my mind.
                Alas
swirled on blue hostas
        glazed with raindrops.
                Alas—too pretty
to be sad though it signifies sadly.
        Alas, the gold finches alight too briefly
                before they migrate to breed.
Alas, the lawn,
        monochrome emblem
                of the love of money,
a single conforming species,
        its rank's blades held aloft,
                poison-tipped,
lethal, alas, to all
        insects (except
                the few pests targeted),
lethal to little helpers
        and food progenitors.
                Alas,
too many mistake for weeds
        and eradicate our wild
                violets and clover.
I like the violet's heart-
        shaped leaves in my salad,
                shining with beads of oil.
I like to think the soil likes
        the clover to fix its nitrogen
                and the clover likes to be the grass

Walt Whitman loves, inviting us to loaf
    and hum among wildflowers
        whose names recall
daughters, home, and harvest—pincushion,
    bachelor's button, and Queen Anne's lace,
        golden rod, cosmos, and prairie aster
sweet alyssum, yarrow, and autumn joy—
    where bees intoxicated by nectar, not toxins,
        live to be our promiscuous pollinators.

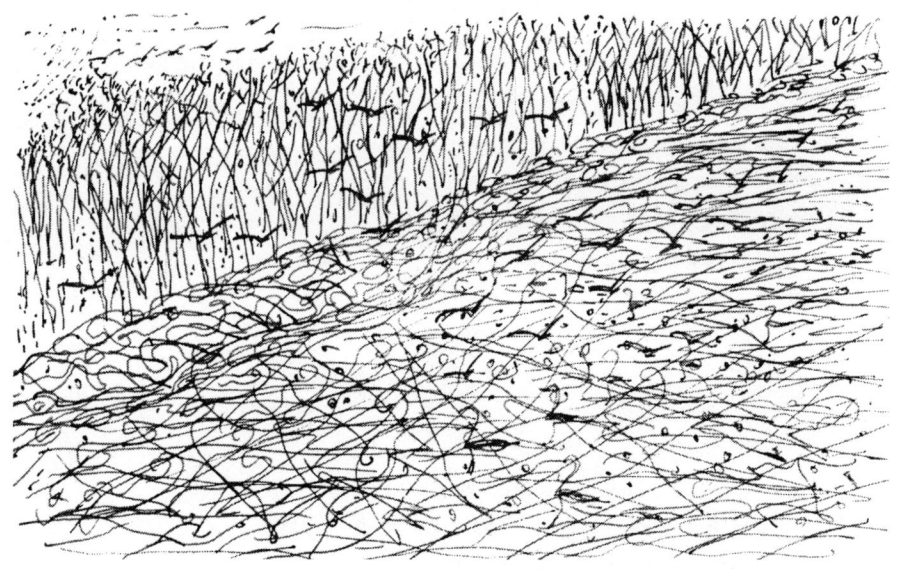

STRANGE

Strange spring of extremes:
        a Mother's Day walk, shedding sleeves,
and overnight, a drop
        of forty degrees;
a picnic of cold vegetables and fruit
        that made us sigh (delicious delight)
gave way to a taste
        for a meal of soup.

Still, my blue-eyed grass opened
        in a storm whose thrashing spread
oak leaf and sweet gumball tree trash
        on the haul we newly spread
on mulched beds, and seedlings
        took a beating from hail the size
of lima beans and peas,
        yet rose again.

I haven't consulted a graph to help me in my belief
        yet grasp that climate chaos
goes beyond the joke—"Don't like the weather?
        Wait five minutes."
Hot poisons pushed an Arctic vortex south,
        then blew past, blew on
and a thaw came too soon, then whirled
        in another freeze.

I complain: "My butterfly bush died—
        for years it gave nectar
for such colorful fluttering joy."
        The garden shop owner replies

grimly: "It was a strange winter."
      I shake my head: "Too many extremes."
I buy a new bush, but not with ease,
      and pray it didn't grow from treated seeds

and the flowers won't dose the honey bees
      with nerve destroyers. I think it strange to ask
and despair how each of us can keep track
      of each link in the chain that supplies our need.

CATS AND DOGS, WHALES AND FROGS

An enormous cloud, I learned,
      weighs as much as two whales
         and yet, as they say, it floats on air.
I suppose a school of whale clouds
      might make a hurricane or tornado
         and what a tragedy if it rained
the poor cats and dogs blown
      from their homes. As for frogs,
         they are good creatures who sing
us to sleep, along with the crickets,
      whippoorwills, and owls,
         even while our plague of poisons
ruins their habitat and they lose
      their organs and can't lay eggs
         or they grow an extra leg.
And if it rains cats and dogs and frogs,
      into warmer and unclean waters,
         the whales forget
where they are or where to go
      or to eat enough to make blubber
         so their hearts won't freeze in the Arctic.
No wonder the whales loudly mourn
      and join in song with a human
         who cares enough to float with them
in a small boat, raise a horn and accompany
      their lament, with only a full moon
         to illumine the ocean.

MOTHER'S DAY AFTER A STORM

Our families gather under a pavilion overlooking the Missouri River,
    the Big Muddy, brown as its nickname, burnished
        with copper and bronze by wind and late spring sun.

The breeze mutes our conversation and our words
    float across the wrought iron tables and our potluck picnic
        (mostly salads) as if they were enclosed in glass globes

or we lean in close to each other's ears, and our hair entwines momentarily.
    She exclaims, "The river's low!" Sandbars and thick tree-roots
        exposed. "Oh, yes!" I call back.

And the sun feels too hot, the bluffs where we perch higher,
    the river below farther from us. The interstate traffic
        on the bridge grows loud like the high wind

of the storm that soaked the ground and dotted our garden beds with hail,
    its tornado fury passing around our town, taking out houses
        to the Northwest and a few daughters and sons.

Every Year the Forget-Me-Nots

Every year the clusters of forget-me-nots
        grow more lush and spread. Admiring
their tiny blossom faces, my daughter and I
        each claim to have cast the original seeds.
Every year I dig up a few to plant in other beds.
        From the living room window I see a spray
of their sky blue each spring, among the bee balm,
        creeping phlox, indigo columbines, violets,
and the dandelions I allow to go to seed
        and become thousands of luminous puffs,
ready to release and reproduce in a breeze.

In another year, my daughter will leave
        our domestic scene, and she no longer cares
much that she helped me plant the fruit trees
        in our backyard. She sits with her friends
and drinks iced tea on the shaded front veranda,
        where the woodland I've created under the oak
gives fragrance to their air, and little yellow
        wild strawberries bloom between the concrete
and the mud near shiny petals, their painted toenails.

Dinner on the Deck with Storms All Around

How calm it is here on our friends' deck,
where we hold hands and each says a few words
to praise the cook, friends, birds at the feeder,

the pasta *al dente* and the asparagus fresh.
A distant tintinnabulation blends
with the greening sky and the soft

conversation. We track the weather
on our gadgets' radar, a tornado to the South
a miles-wide swath of storm to the West—

yet agitation doesn't figure in our calculations.
After dinner, ten-year-old Ruth jokes,
"We're all going to die!" Her dad smiles,

"One day, yes. Probably not tonight.
Why don't you stay at the table with our friend
and write a poem before your bedtime?"

WOODLANDS PSALM
—for Ellis Froechle, who walks with me

O, Botanist in the Highest, help me bow
       and bend in awe over white flowers
       dangling from the stems of Solomon's Seal
       like miniature pairs of slippers.
Help me identify the Barren Strawberry,
       Wild Ginger, Stars of Bethlehem,
       sky-blue flowering Jacob's Ladder,
       Larkspur, and the Zigzag Spiderwort,
       related to the Wandering Jew;
       those You made native to these forests.
Let me join with the righteous who fight
       the woodland's enemies: Kudzu
       and Bradford Pear, and the Exotic
       Bush Honeysuckle, an ornamental
       displaced for lawns (now endangered
       at home in Japan), whose seed
       is spread by innocent birds, who need
       to eat and excrete.
Protect my skin and let me see
       the Poison Ivy leaf's oily sheen;
       let me know better than to touch
       the Stinging Nettle.
Let my voice call out, Hallelujah, hallelujah!
       for the multitudes of Milkweed
       standing tall for the Monarch
       butterflies, risen on banks of wetlands
       fed by the Missouri River and Moniteau Creek.
Walk beside us when my friend and I stroll a path
       lined with Horsetail, living fossils
       from Paleozoic forests; and she shows
       how the ancient rushes' stalks can be broken
       into whistles, each with a different tone.

Let us keep the memory that Moniteau is the Algonquin
        name for the Great Spirit when we sight
        a Little Blue Heron, its arching neck and oval body
        forming a quarter note we can see in Your composition;
        and we are as still as the sun and the elegant bird
        mirrored on glowing waters, exalting You.

Isis in Missouri

President Obama: We will 'degrade and destroy' ISIS
—MSNBC headline 9/3/14

My brown-skinned Isis listens
    to the prayers of slaves and artisans.
Sunday afternoon I visit my friends
    in the village of Rocheport.
Kent's cooked Egyptian lentils and roasted
    tomatoes with eggs rolled in *duqqa*
he's made by grinding hazelnuts, sea salt flakes,
    coriander, cumin, and nigella seeds.
I bow my head over the bowl of aromas
    rising delectable enough for goddesses
and gods who are nourished, smelling the food
    we humans eat. All day Isis's name is
on my tongue, a grain of fennel sweetening
    my breath when I speak.
Isis riding the airwaves. Isis is with us as we wander
    the KATY trail where the old train tracks
used to run from border to border, sometimes
    along the Big Muddy River,
and sometimes across the wide prairies where once
    only herds of hoofed creatures trampled
the grasses and wildflowers, until big cats
    and wolves took them down,
the same way as somewhere in Africa. Now the wild
    animals and the savannas are fenced in.
The weeping willow is cascading green light
    sparkling Isis's name without fear.
The air is perfect and smooths our skin like water,
    and everyone on the path
smiles with peace to be walking with family or biking
    through the tunnel into radiant trees.
All day long Isis appears, mother with child, icon
    passed generation to generation, faith to faith.

Across the wetlands a huge turtle warms its shell,
        perched on a log, attended by dragonflies
hovering, reflecting blues and greens, sky and water.
        We stop to chat with the owners
of an outdoor pizzeria and bakery.
        Their daughter sits on a wrought iron throne,
nursing her baby beneath the canopy of a vast mulberry.
        Sparrows eat crumbs at our feet.
The afternoon sun disk is caught in a sycamore,
        two white branches sticking out
like cow's horns, and vultures circle above Moniteau Creek.
        She does not hide her full breast,
as the group of us talk about books and food,
        the decline of the bees and Monarchs.
We do not take God the Mother's name in vain
        to mean terror; we do not seek
to degrade and destroy her brown skin.

A Mother At Midnight

Let her be with friends on the bank lush with cattails,
        bulrushes, marsh milkweed, and willows.
Let her be laughing, her head thrown back, her lungs
        swelling with good oxygen.
Let her sprawl on the dock and lean against
        the living body of air.
Keep her from the dark river.
Keep her from the invisible currents.

Hummingbird Home

Real estate agents talk about "homes for sale"
      and misuse the word. If you could buy home,
            then *home* is senseless, just as God is not

defined except by those who by defining undo the divine—
      or who won't love the wings they cannot see.
            The hummingbird attracted to the red feeder

could no longer delight if I held him still,
      examined the details of his poor wings crushed
            in my grasp. Framed in one of the twelve times

two panes, he hovers in tiny fractions of the hours—
      my friend who loves math might call his flight a fractal,
            which I don't understand though I've leaned awed

toward the screen to see their morphing beauty
      graphically animated. He shows himself briefly,
            his translucent wings too-fast-to-see blending

with the sky and lake turning pink and red
      (his favorite colors) and he swerves—such speed—
            in and out of our dining room view on a day

too hot to swim, even for teenagers, even on Friday
      in July. We've made a home for the hummingbirds,
            with the sugar water my love boils, cools,

then pours into red plastic, a cheerful ersatz flower
      for hummingbirds to be nectar drunk,
            while other birds peck at our other feeders.

I hope for home for them, too, and, gloveless,
      dirt lining my fingernails like kohl, pushed into the earth
            some mammoth sunflower seeds, for sparrows,

chickadees, cardinals, and goldfinches to enter dizzying yellow
and feed on homegrown rich black seeds at the center.
This home the real estate agent didn't find for us—

a friend saw the sign. My dream to live on water—
my daughter proclaimed was ours—
"This is our home, Mommy." We stood together

beneath the oak on an evening almost as humid as now, looking
at the few lights scribbling indecipherable names on the lake.
This place my kid will leave too soon for me

but just right for her, as it was for me, who could not call
my hometown—or any one place—home.
My story won't be hers, I pray. Most summer days

she and her friends sling towels over their shoulders,
and single-file cross out of our yard to the lake,
their wings invisible, on their route of evanescence.

All the poems in *Dwelling* that refer to environmental destruction, including climate change, are based on science.

"Eat God": "*Do this for the remembrance of me*" is a fragment from the liturgy. The Eucharistic Prayer in the Episcopal *Book of Common Prayer* quotes from the accounts of The Last Supper in Luke 22:19-20 and 1 Corinthians 11:24-25. "The peace that passes understanding" Philippians 4-7 is a closing blessing at the end of the Holy Eucharist. "Enigmatic mirror" at the end of the poem refers to the well-known passage in I Corinthians 13:12, when St. Paul writes in the King James translation: "For now we see through a glass darkly, but then face to face." In his translation, *The Restored New Testament*, Willis Barnstone translates "see through a glass darkly" from Koine Greek as "look into an enigmatic mirror."

"The House my Great-Grandfather Built": My great-grandparents immigrated from what, in the 1880s, was Imperial Russia. Family history holds that Hyman "Mike" Lempert was the first Jew to immigrate to Lewiston-Auburn from their village. My grandmother, Dora Lempert Barnstone was the daughter of Hyman and Sarah Halperin [Gelperin, Alpren, Alperen] Lempert. Sarah and my other Jewish great-grandfather, Morris Barnstone, née Bornstein, were first cousins. Having studied the family tree, I surmise that we're related to every Jew with roots in the area. Though Maine has an ugly history of anti-Semitic and anti-immigrant Nativism, historically, Maine's Twin Cities, Lewiston-Auburn, boast a thriving Jewish Community. Perhaps the presence of Bates College in Lewiston, founded in 1855 by Free Will Baptist Abolitionists, made the community more welcoming; Bates was co-ed from the beginning and allowed admission to all qualified students, regardless of race or creed. For more see Documenting Maine Jewry, www.mainejews.org.

"Name Change": In January 1782, the Austrian Emperor Joseph II's "Edict of Tolerance" required that all Jews take German name. In Luke 2:1-5, as decreed by Caesar Augustus, Joseph and Mary go to Bethlehem to register and be taxed. My grandfather, born Robert Bornstein, convinced his father, step-mother, and all his siblings to change the family name to Barnstone, in 1912, Auburn, Maine.

"Collage with Bread and Roses": "What the woman who labors wants is the right to live, not simply exist—the right to life as the rich woman has the right to life, and the sun and music and art. You have nothing that the humblest worker has not a right to have also. The worker must have bread, but she must have roses, too" is from Rose Schneiderman's "Bread and Roses" speech (1911). It is said that her speech inspired the poem "Bread and Roses" by James Oppenheim, but it may also be the reverse. The poem, "Bread and Roses," was set to music by Mimi Fariña (1974).

"My Greek Grandmother's Hunger": My mother and her family are survivors of the German occupation of Greece, one of the most brutal. All told, 13% of the Greek population was killed by the Germans, including 70,000 Jews. The historian Mark Mazower writes that somewhere between a quarter and a half a million Greeks died of starvation during the German imposed famine.

"Meadows and Fireflies": Fireflies are disappearing all over the world because of habitat destruction, pesticides, and light pollution. People who have yards can help by not using pesticides, not mowing an area so tall grasses and flowers grow, and turning off lights at night.

"When We Were Girls in Goshen": Abigail Stone, Ruth Stone's daughter, is the author of *Recipes from the Dump* (W.W. Norton, 1995). Ruth Stone (1915-2011) was a renowned poet.

"Hymn for my Bird": The epigraph is from Anne Bradstreet's poem, "In Reference to her Children, 23 June 1659."

"My Greek Grandmother with my Bird and at the Piano": My grandmother, Maria Tzalopoulou, was a trained pianist, soprano, and actress. Her father, Haralambos Agniades, was the Sultana's lawyer in Istanbul (which most Greeks still call Constantinople or "the City").

"Monkey Mind Goes to Fetch Something": My paternal grandfather, Robert Barnstone, aka R.C. Barnstone (1893-1946) was a visionary businessman, who specialized in diamonds, Swiss watches, and, at the end of his life, Mexican silver. He divorced my grandmother, Dora Lempert Barnstone (who was his second cousin), moved to Colorado Springs, began importing Mexican silver, and married a young Mexican Sephardic Jew, Marti Franco. He jumped off a Colorado Springs building and is buried in the Sons of Israel Cemetery in Colorado Springs, far from the family plot Beth Jacob Cemetery in Auburn, which I describe in "The House my Great-Grandfather Built." Two of my uncles, Howard Barnstone (1923-1987) and Robert Barnstone (1946-2008), who took after their father in brilliance, vision, and charm, also killed themselves.

"In the Workshop": The Mario Savio Steps of Sproul Hall on the campus of the University of California, Berkeley, are named for Savio, who was an activist and prominent member of the Free Speech Movement. "Then, there are certain states you get into with opium, and heroin, of almost disembodied awareness, looking down back at the Earth from a place after you're dead." Allen Ginsberg interviewed by Thomas Clark in *The Paris Review, The Art of Poetry No. 8.*

"Who Knew How Far": The poem refers to C.P. Cavafy's "The City."

"I Was Sick and You Visited Me": Matthew 25:42. "Snow on snow" is from Christina Rossetti's poem, "In the Bleak Midwinter," which is also a Christmas carol.

"Of a New Year's Eve": "passion map": the title of one of Adrianne Kalfopoulou's books of poetry is Passion Maps.

"Goose Rush": Geese are very intelligent creatures, with good memories. Because of "imprinting," goslings can be trained to believe that human beings are their family.

"Well" and "Elegy in the Second Person": Cliff Becker (1964-2005) was a dear friend. He was the Literature Director of the National Endowment for the Arts NEA's literary director, oversaw NEA grants to literary organizations and individual writers and translators. He expanded support for individual translators at the agency and led the development of the NEA Literature Translation Initiative. Other national initiatives in which he played a leading role include the Favorite Poem Project, the Literary Journal Institute and the National Poetry Recitation Contest.

"At the End of Your Life": Throughout the poem there are quotations from Emily Dickinson's poems and letters. ED's "abolitionist friend" is Thomas Wentworth Higginson. Rabbi Isaac Luria (1534-1572). "[L]oose the stop from your throat" Walt Whitman, "Song of Myself," line 76. Biblical references: *Love as strong as death*, Song of Solomon 8:6; [become like little children] *to enter the kingdom of heaven*, Matthew 18:3-4 & Mark 10:15; *stones cry out*, Habakkuk 2:11 & Luke 19:40, *way into the wilderness*, Isaiah 43:19; *consider the lilies of the field*, Matthew 6:28 & Luke 12:27; *abide in me as I abide in you*, John 15:4-7; *I was sick and you visited me*, Matthew 25:42; *be of good cheer*, John 16:33.

"Residential Geese": Sadly, the neighborhood association eradicated the goose population of the lake by painting their eggs, thus depriving those of us who love the birds of their delightfully comic behavior, their humbling intelligence, and their magnificent beauty. The association replaced the geese with ducks. Now we can no longer swim in the lake because of "swimmer's itch" or duck parasites.

"The Great Along": Michael S. Harper (1938-2016) was my beloved professor when I was a student at Brown University. The title is taken from the last line of MSH's poem, "Songbirds (Habitat)" in *Use Trouble*. In an interview on Terry Gross's *Fresh Air*, he said: "the most important thing you learn from musicians is phrasing. And you learn it from the singers - you know, the Bessie Smiths, the Billie Holidays, the Mamie Smiths, the Aretha Franklins even. But you also learn, more than anything else, about the authenticity of phrasing because musicians take you to places that you might not necessarily want to go. And they go instantly to the transcendent and of course the mastery of their playing is not technical mastery. It is spiritual mastery. It is to take you to a place that perhaps is not your mode. And when we are in performance with musicians, they take us to places sometimes we don't want to go. We're not prepared to go. They take us instantly there." The poem alludes to Robert Hayden's "Those Winter Sundays" and John Coltraine's "A Love Supreme."

"Saunter *Sans Terre*": The poem quotes Henry David Thoreau's "Walking" and "Civil Disobedience."

"Windows on the Past": The biblical quotations are from Hebrews 12:1.

"A Little More Mindful": The biblical accounts of Palm Sunday are found in Matthew 21:1-11, Mark 11:1-11, Luke 19:28-44, and John 12:12-19. Luke 19:42 Jesus says, "If only you knew on this day those things creating peace." (The translation is Willis Barnstone's.) Jesus's seamless robe appears in John 19:23. In some traditions, the Virgin Mary wove Jesus's seamless robe, and he wore it his whole life; symbolically, Mary clothed Jesus in flesh. For more on Athena and story-cloths see Evy Johanne Håland, "Athena's Peplos: Weaving as a Core Female Activity in Ancient and Modern Greece," *Cosmos: The journal of the Traditional Cosmology Society* 20, 2006: 155-182.

"Gethsemane Psalm": "And when they had sung a hymn, they went out to the Mount of Olives" (Matthew 26:30; Mark 14:26). The hymn, which I call "the closing psalm," would have been derived from the Hallel Psalms or "Praise" Psalims (113-118), sung at the end of Seder. Many scholars hold that the Last Supper was a Seder. Though there would have been no Haggadah in Jesus's time, in Exodus God commands Jews to tell to "children and grandchildren" the story of the Lord's intervention that freed them from slavery in Egypt. (See Exodus 10:2 and 13:8.) "Stay awake..." (Matthew 25:15). "I am the way…" John 14:6. Golgotha "means the place of the skull" (Matthew 27:33).

"Holy Friday": The poem refers to the Legend of the Dogwood and to the icons of the "Harrowing of Hell," in which Jesus is depicted raising Adam and Eve from their tombs. Jesus frequently calls on his followers to give up their riches and care for the poor; in Luke 16:19-25 Jesus warns that greed and disregard for the poor, the sick, and needy will be punished with hell. As a Rabbi, Jesus was reiterating the central commandment or mitzvah of Judaism to love your neighbor as yourself and to care for those less fortunate than yourself. "Tzedakah" is usually translated as "charity," but a more accurate translation is "righteousness" or "justice." For the righteous, tzedakah is a duty, a requirement, not an act of generosity.

"Alas": "The love of money" is from 1 Timothy 6:10: "For the love of money is the root of all evil: which while some coveted after, they have erred from the faith, and pierced themselves through with many sorrows." This scripture has its antecedent in many verses in the Old Testament. For example, these lines from Job echo Timothy: "If I have made gold my hope, or have said to the fine gold, Thou art my confidence.... This also were an iniquity to be punished by the judge: for I should have denied the God that is above" (Job 31:24-28). For more, see above, "Holy Friday."

"Strange": There is a large body of scientific evidence showing that seeds treated with neonicotinoids are responsible of honey-bee colony collapse disorder and are toxic to other pollinators, birds, aquatic invertebrates, and wildlife.

"Woodlands Psalm": "Hallelujah, hallelujah! / for the multitudes of Milkweed / standing tall for the Monarch / butterflies": like the fireflies the monarchs are disappearing because of human encroachment, specifically, the destruction of milkweed, which is necessary for the survival of the monarchs; they lay their eggs on milkweed and eat it, which makes them poisonous to their predators.

"Isis in Missouri": The work I did for my edition of H.D.'s *Trilogy* heightens my awareness of the use and misuse of names, particularly the names of female deities. Isis is the Hellenized form of "Aset" or "Iset." I call her God the Mother because, as H.D. shows, the depictions of Isis suckling her son Horus carry forward in the Christian iconography of Mary and the baby Jesus. Her divinity encompasses more than I can enumerate here; she is the Egyptian Goddess of motherhood, fertility, wisdom, health, magic, healing, death, rebirth, and marriage. "Isis" means throne. Some of the symbols of Isis that appear in this poem include cow's horns with the sun disk between them, the cow, sparrows, and the vulture. President Obama never refers to the terrorist group as ISIS but as ISIL.

"Hummingbird Home": The last phrase, "a route of evanescence" is the first line of Emily Dickinson's poem about a hummingbird.

NO LONGER THE PROPERTY OF
THE ST. LOUIS COUNTY LIBRARY